THE FALCON SOARS

THE FALCON SOARS

Bowling Green State University: The Years of Growing Distinction 1963-1985

Stuart R. Givens

Bowling Green State University Popular Press
Bowling Green, Ohio 43403

DEDICATION

To my wife, Florence, and Bowling Green
State University, both of whom I have had
the pleasure of sharing much of my life.

CONTENTS

PREFACE

The genesis of this book was a request by President Hollis A. Moore in 1980 that the author write as part of the Seventy-Fifth Anniversary a supplement to Dr. Overman's history of the first fifty years of Bowling Green State University. In order that the last quarter century be seen as a part of a continuing evolution of the university, a brief survey of the first fifty years has been given.

The author has attempted to survey more fully the history of the university beginning with the presidency of William Jerome in 1963. As is the case always, the process has been selective, and, therefore, a number of events have been ignored or lightly touched upon. The author hopes that despite whatever shortcomings there might be, the essence of Bowling Green and its history has been caught.

The archival resources available for research on the university for the past twenty five years are overwhelming. Consequently, the author limited himself to some of the major collections. Those sources are the ones that appear regularly in the endnotes. One bit of caution on sources needs be mentioned. The numbering of the *BG News* is not reliable, and hence if one wants to look up a reference he should use the date rather than the volume and issue number.

In the process of researching and writing over the past five years the author has become deeply indebted in various ways to a number of people. I would like to thank for their encouragement Hollis A. Moore, Richard A. Edwards, Michael R. Ferrari, and Paul J. Olscamp. Of particular help in searching out materials was the University Archivist Ann Bowers. In addition, Judy Robins and Paul Yon of the Center for Archival Collections rendered service beyond that necessary. The CAC and Richard J. Wright of the Institute for Great Lakes Research provided a corner of their facilities that allowed both proximity to materials and the privacy necessary to work. In addition, Rick Wright extended many courtesies that are deeply appreciated.

One last group needs to be recognized—those who have helped with the publication of the book. The support of Larry Weiss and the Alumni Association has been of invaluable worth. In the actual organizing of the final product Clif Boutelle and Deb McLaughlin of the Office of Public Relations and Pat and Ray Browne of the Popular Press have steered, with inordinate patience, the author through the intricacies of book production.

The semester's leave granted by the university made the completion of the project close to on time possible. The author would like to thank, also, the many colleagues and friends who nagged, prodded, cajoled, and humored him over the years. Finally, I must thank my wife, Florence, for her forebearance and patience.

SECTION I
PROLOGUE

CHAPTER I

A UNIVERSITY IS CREATED
The First Fifty Years - An Overview

CHAPTER I

The First Fifty Years
The Beginnings

The year 1910 was a year of special importance for the people of northern Ohio. On the tenth of May the state legislature enacted the Lowry Bill which provided for the "establishment of two additional state normal schools, one in northeastern Ohio and one in northwestern Ohio,...".[1] On November 10th of that year Bowling Green was chosen as the site for the normal school in the northwest. The City of Bowling Green had campaigned diligently along with sixteen other communities to be the location of the new school. The city had offered the selecting commission four different sites including the city park and surrounding lots totaling eighty-two and a half acres - the one finally chosen.[2]

The Lowry Act mandated the establishment of a five member Board of Trustees for each of the two schools. Governor Judson Harmon in the Spring of 1911 appointed such a board for Bowling Green which subsequently in late June met and elected officers. The primary concern of the board during its first several months of existence was the choice of a president for the institution. In spite of considerable political pressure the trustees chose in 1912 a man with high professional qualifications and experience—Homer B. Williams, Superintendent of Schools in Sandusky.

The second major task facing the trustees, and now President Williams, was the development of a physical plant. With monetary authorization for two buildings the architectural firm of Howard and Merriam of Columbus began planning a classroom building and a dormitory. In the Spring of 1913 ground was broken for the first building, the Administration

Building (University Hall). The original plans were expanded when in 1913 the legislature appropriated almost one and half million dollars instead of the anticipated total of two hundred and fifty thousand. The revised scheme called for four buildings — the general classroom (University Hall), a dormitory (Williams), a Science and Agriculture structure (Moseley), and a heating plant (Centrex Building).[3]

President Williams was faced with several other challenges, among which were the locating and hiring of a faculty and the determination of a proper curriculum. Between the Fall of 1913 and the opening of classes in September, 1914, Williams employed ten faculty members and four critic teachers. Only two of the faculty had taught in northwest Ohio and, while prepared professionally, none held a doctoral degree. The Board of Trustees and the President were authorized by the Lowry Act to develop a curriculum suited to both the theoretical and the practical needs of students desiring to teach. They determined that the immediate need was for a two-year diploma program and a one-year plan for rural teachers, but that provision should be made to allow for expansion to a four year degree program. This was most clearly demonstrated by the conscious decision to name the school Bowling Green State Normal College instead of Normal School—a term which implied two-year degree programs only. One other major determination made prior to the opening of the college was that the basis for admission would be graduation from an accredited four-year high school. The intent of this provision was to safeguard the academic reputation of a fledgling institution.[4]

The First Years

Dear Alma Mater staunch and true—We pledge our heart and hand for you—No other school so grand has e'er been seen as Normal College Bowling Green[5]

In the Fall of 1914 Bowling Green opened its doors to 304 full time students, fifty-eight of whom were men. The student body was composed of individuals from thirty one different counties in Ohio and with one student each from Michigan and New York. Two thirds of them were from Wood and Lucas counties, and, unlike later years, none were residents of Cuyahoga County. In addition to the on-campus students, the faculty taught twice as many students in extension classes. During the first year with the campus buildings unfinished, all classes in Bowling Green were held in the National Guard Armory while the weekly convocations and the library were housed across the corner in the Methodist Church. The summer of 1915 saw the first summer classes double the enrollment of the first year, thus demonstrating clearly that there was a desire for the upgrading of teaching credentials on the part of teachers and school systems.

The curriculum available the initial year covered thirteen subjects: agriculture, biological science, education, english, geography, history, home economics, industrial arts, library, mathematics, music, physical education, and physical science all taught by a total of ten faculty members.

This new institution was situated on the east side of a town of approximately six thousand whose "... citizens are deeply interested in the welfare of the College, and in which...the educational and moral tone of the community is wholesome and helpful in the highest degree." Moreover, the first catalog continued, "The climate of Bowling Green is favorable to study, extremes of temperature being modified by the proximity of Lake Erie."[6] The town was easily accessible since it was served by two north-south railroads and north-south and east-west electric interurban lines.

The Dormitory for Women and the Administration Building were ready for use when school began in the Fall of 1915. They were located on a campus of eighty-two and a half acres which was considered more than adequate for years to come. By the time cold weather arrived the new heating plant was also operational.

President Charles W. Eliot of Harvard once said that a new institution could emulate an old one in most respects, but that it had to grow its own ivy. Bowling Green initiated that process almost immediately. During the first year three elements of tradition evolved—the choice of school colors, the composing of an alma mater, and the designing of a college seal. Leon L. Winslow, Head of Industrial Arts, was instrumental in deciding on the colors (burnt orange and seal brown) and personally designed the seal, while Ernest G. Hesser of Music composed "We Hail You, Dear Normal College." Professor Winslow sparked the founding during that inaugural year, as well, of the oldest continuing organization at Bowling Green —Book and Motor—now known as Phi Kappa Phi. While other traditions were still to come, the first year did much to start the ivy.[8]

A University Evolves

Forty-eight years elapsed between the Fall of 1915 and the beginning of the administration of William T. Jerome III as the sixth President. During that span the country and the university experienced two world wars and the Great Depression. These events resulted in a nation and an institution which was quite different. The evolution while convoluted at times was toward a larger, more complex organism.

The People

While ideas are the heart of a university and organization, curriculum and activities the sinew—the people are the body, Over the first fifty years of its life Bowling Green grew from a student body of 304 to 7617. The sex mix changed over that period from a predominantly female, to a heavily male, to a balanced one. When classes began on campus in 1915 the student body was eighty-one percent female. By 1931 that had dropped to seventy-six percent, and then in 1943 at the height of World War II shot up to ninety-two percent. At the peak of the veterans' bulge in 1949 sixty-four percent of the student body was male, but by 1962 it had declined to fifty-five percent. During that time span the total enrollment of the university grew slowly but steadily. The figures by decades were: 1915 - 304, 1925 - 798, 1935 - 1042, 1945 - 1668, 1955 - 3635, and 1965 - 9030. The only variance from the pattern was the aberration caused by World War II when in 1943 there were only 829 students registered.[9]

As would be expected the faculty grew in size generally in relation to the student body. In the Fall of 1915 there were sixteen faculty members on campus plus several critic teachers — none of whom held a doctoral degree. By 1929 those figures were forty-eight faculty, eight percent of whom had a Ph.D.. During the decade of the 1930's, the institution now named

Bowling Green State College, doubled its faculty to eighty five and dramatically increased the number holding the doctorate to sixty four percent. The loss of faculty during World War II and the need in the immediate post-war period to meet the demands of the veterans enrollment led to a marked increase in the faculty, but a dramatic drop in the percentage holding a doctorate. The figures of 1950-51 were 233, of which only twenty-one percent were doctorates. The McDonald years — the 1950's — witnessed an interesting anomaly in the growth pattern. During that period the total faculty increased by only twenty-one persons, but the percentage with a Ph.D. moved from twenty one to sixty-one percent. Needless to say, in 1961 fifty-eight percent of the faculty were new since 1951.[10]

One other vital human element in the life of an institution of higher learning is its leadership—the President and the Board of Trustees. Five men served Bowling Green as President during the first fifty years of classes: Homer B. Williams (1912-1937), Roy E. Offenhauer (1937-1938), Frank J. Prout (1939-1951), Ralph W. McDonald (1951-1961), and Ralph G. Harshman (1961-1963). That same period found thirty-six individuals serving on the Board of Trustees which to almost the very end was composed of five members. Of the thirty-six, three were women and ten served for at least a decade. Six of the board played a sustaining part in the governance of Bowling Green in that they served twenty or more years. Four of them, Alva W. Bachman, James C. Donnell II, E. Tappan Rodgers, and Carl H. Schwyn, served almost concurrently from the middle of the 1940's until the mid-1960's.[11]

Organization and Curriculum

The inter-war period of 1918-1941 saw the emergence of a university in name and structure. In 1928-1929, with slightly over 950 students in attendance, the state legislature approved the change in status of Bowling Green State Normal College to Bowling Green State College with the right to grant a baccalaureate degree. With that authority, the Board of Trustees approved the creation of a College of Liberal Arts. Six years later the legislature authorized a further name change to that of

Bowling Green State University. The Board followed that action with the formation of a College of Business and approval of a limited Masters level graduate program. Thus in title Bowling Green by the outbreak of World War II was a university.

Interestingly, the growth of the institution occurred partially in spite of the intentions of the state. The Emmons-Hanna Act of 1929 did not authorize the creation of a new college, but only the offering of a four-year degree. President Williams and the Board used that authorization as permission to add the College of Liberal Arts. The very existence of the college was endangered in the depths of the depression. In 1933 the Senate Finance Committee proposed to close down Bowling Green and convert its buildings for the use of a mental institution. President Williams, many faculty and townspeople vigorously opposed this suggestion, and by organizing the Northwestern Ohio Educational Protective Association carried out an effective lobbying campaign that kept the college intact. After 1935 the life of Bowling Green was assured.

As indicated in the name Bowling Green was a university by 1939, but organizationally it remained a large college. From 1914 until 1929 the institution was a college which was headed by a Dean of Instruction and the President. With the creation in 1929 of two colleges a further organizational division seemed natural, but could not be worked out. The two deans who superseded the Dean of Instruction agreed to a general division of the instructional departments, but concurred that on critical issues consensus was necessary. When a third college was added in 1935 the need for reorganization became even more apparent, but differences continued over how to divide the faculty functionally when most of them were in liberal arts but the majority of students were in education. Since no logical solution seemed possible, an arbitrary division was made which placed approximately one third of the then seventeen departments equally under the three deans. This pattern held until 1951 when the structure which has continued largely to the present was devised; one that generally placed departments within colleges where they academically most logically belonged.

The last ingredient added that made Bowling Green a university occurred in 1935 with the authorization of graduate degrees.

Initially only a Master of Arts was available, and at the end of World War II it was awarded in only eight areas. The next six years saw a rapid increase in graduate programs so by the early 1950's four different masters degrees in nineteen disciplines were offered. This growth entailed some organizational changes as well. From 1935 to 1947 the graduate program was supervised by a committee and the deans. In 1947 the Graduate School was organized and placed under a director. Four years later the director was elevated to being a dean. At the very end of the first fifty years that last step in graduate education was taken. In 1960 the Board of Trustees gave permission for planning doctoral degrees in biology, education, English, and speech. This led to authorization of a Ph.D. in English — the first two of which were granted in January, 1963.[12]

Curricular offerings expanded over the years as the nature of the school changed. When classes began on campus there were fourteen basic course combinations available running from 16 classes in agriculture and industrial arts through eleven in Latin and nine in German to three in Biology. A decade later in 1924 the total course offerings had only increased by one and the classes offered did not vary greatly except that German had been dropped and replaced by French and Spanish. By 1936 with the creation of two new colleges completed the total curricular offerings grew slightly, but the actual number of courses expanded dramatically. While agriculture continued to be offered, it had dropped to seven classes and ceased being offered after 1938. Meanwhile, courses in History and Mathematics doubled in number and the newcomer Business Administration placed forty three courses in the catalog. The development of the graduate program and the expanded post war enrollments contributed to a more than doubling of disciplines to forty by 1952, accompanied by a marked increase in individual courses. The 1950's saw a slight decline in both, as faculty growth was held almost constant.[13]

Concomitant with the greater variety of course offerings was an increase in academic departments. In 1914 there were thirteen departments, a number of which offered courses in more than one subject. During the next fifty years departments evolved along two major lines. The first of them reflected clearly the

creation of two new colleges. The second avenue stemmed from
the need to further refine along departmental lines burgeoning
disciplines. This pattern occurred in the evolution from a Social
Science Department to departments of Economics, History,
Political Science, Psychology, and Sociology, and similarly
from English to Journalism and Speech. Statistically this evolution was as follows: 1914 - 13 departments; 1929 - 16 departments; 1939 -20 departments; and 1952 until 1963 - 30 departments.[14]

Another indication of the changing and growing curriculum
was to be seen in the library and its holdings. The original
library was a small room in the Methodist Church and then a
larger room (303 Administration Building). The collection size
in 1916 was approximately 10,000 volumes which several
catalogs assured students was a "...well selected list of books
and periodicals..."[15] In 1939 the library, for over a decade in a
separate building, had 45,000 volumes which grew to 188,000
by 1951 and 330,000 by the early 1960s.[16]

A further reflection of growth and the changing curriculum
was the enrollment distribution and the degrees awarded during
the first fifty years. From 1914 until the 1930s all students were
registered in education and received either a two-year diploma
or a bachelor's degree. The last two-year diploma was given in
1939 at which time a total of 4,002 had been granted as com-
pared with 1,473 baccalaureates. Most of the bachelor's degrees
through the 1930s were for secondary teaching, with the first
one in the liberal arts being given in 1931 and in business administration in 1937. By the beginning of World War II the
variance in enrollment resulting from university status emerged.
The 1939-40 academic year found thirty-five percent of the
undergraduate students outside of the College of Education
while by 1949-50 that figure had risen to fifty-six percent, and by
the early 1960s it stood at forty-eight percent. Concomitant with
the increase in enrollment in the liberal arts and business was a
slower but real one at the graduate level. Only nine students
were registered for graduate degrees in 1945 but by 1950 the
number had climbed to 198 only to dip during the 1950s before
an upturn in the early 1960s to 328. One other reflection of the
growing and changing role of graduate education was in the

number of degrees awarded. In 1945 a total of eighty-eight master's degrees had been bestowed—a figure that grew to 1868 by 1963—plus by that year nine Specialist and two doctoral degrees.[17]

College Life

We wave high our banner Your the commander, Orange and brown float high Rah! Rah![18]

While a number of the symbols of tradition emerged during the first year or so several more evolved over the next decades. A number of these centered around athletics such as the first homecoming in 1922 and the naming by Ivan Lake of the falcon as a mascot in 1927. Another traditional fixture appeared in 1946 with the birth of the pep organization SICSIC. It has dotted the campus with its signs ever since.[19]

A variety of student organizations blossomed over the first fifty years. As noted earlier, the first year witnessed the start of literary and honorary societies. Over the next several years departmental and interest groups were created. Among the earliest of these were musical organizations such as the women's chorus—Treble Clef, an orchestra, and in 1923 a band.

It was not until the second decade of the school that the first national honorary, Phi Sigma Mu (Music) was founded. During the time leading up to World War II it was joined by Pi Kappa Delta (Forensics), Beta Pi Theta (French), Sigma Tau Delta (English), Sigma Delta Psi (Athletics), Kappa Mu Epsilon (Mathematics), and Kappa Delta Pi (Education). The post war years and the 1950's witnessed these seven mushrooming to thirty.

Student publications were started early but failed, only to be reattempted. The forerunner of the *BG News* was the ten-issue a year monthly that first appeared in 1920 as the *Bee Gee News* which in time developed into a weekly. A college annual was also published early in the form of the 1918 *THE BEEGEE,* but it folded after one year. In the fall of 1923 a group of students gained permission to attempt publishing another yearbook. It appeared late in the spring of 1924 under the title of *The Key.* Over the years a number of other publications have been attempted but only these first two of the first fifty years have endured.[20]

Bowling Green while not conceived of as a residential school, ironically or maybe prophetically, opened in 1915 with only a classroom building and a dormitory completed. In the first year the residents of the hall formed a Hall Board—an idea that was duplicated as further dormitories opened. In 1916 a group of men formed a secret social group called Theta Delta Chi which led a tenuous existence but through various name changes still exists. In the early 1920's a few more social groups were formed including in 1923 the first two women's organizations —Five Sisters and Skol. By the end of World War II a sizeable number of social clubs existed with quarters in a number of small university built and owned "cottages". President Prout approved during the war the entry of national fraternal groups on the campus. This resulted in 1942 in the chartering of the Commoners as a chapter of Pi Kappa Alpha and in 1943 of Delhi (a factional descendant of Theta Delta Chi) as a chapter of Alpha Tau Omega. That same year the first national sorority came on campus in the form of Alpha Xi Delta which had been Five Sisters. At the time of Dr. Prout's retirement the number of social groups had risen to fifteen fraternities and eleven sororities all but one of which was a national affiliate. Overman in his history said that "Bringing these strong national organizations to the University was the accomplishment of which President Prout was most proud."[21] It certainly did change the nature of the university.

The hall board of Williams Hall was indicative of a pattern of student involvement that grew gradually over the first fifty years. During the first year on campus a Social Committee was created with the charge to oversee all-college social events. The committee included students on it. In 1917-18 when the Athletic Committee was formed students were again members. The first move toward student government occurred in 1922 with the founding of the Women's League to help in developing policy for all women students. During the latter years of President Williams' administration and the whole of Dr. Prout's the trend continued. In 1931 an inter-fraternity and an inter-sorority council appeared, followed in 1936 by the University Student's Association of which all students were members. By 1951 students not only had their own governing bodies but were represented on all university committees that dealt with student activities. The McDonald years witnessed further growth with the creation of the Student Court and the Council on Student Affairs. In the late 50s the Student Senate, the legislative body of the USA, wrote a new constitution which reconstituted it as the Student Body Organization. One other form of liaison among administration, faculty, and students during the first fifty years was the university assembly. For the first thirty years they were required and held weekly, but during the last twenty they became less frequent and finally died entirely by 1960.[22]

In the United States the interrelatedness of college life and athletics by the 20th century had become almost axiomatic. Hence it is not surprising that athletic teams were formed early in the life of Bowling Green. Since during the first fifty years all intercollegiate athletic teams were male, the first several years found Bowling Green operating at a disadvantage with its low male enrollment. Even so, in 1916 F.G. Beyerman organized a basketball team which played eight games. This was followed by baseball — 1918, football —1919, tennis and track — 1922, and cross country —1927. While until the 1940s Bowling Green did not become well known athletically it did make the national record book in 1921 when it defeated Findlay College in football 151-0. The coming in 1942 of Harold Anderson to Bowling Green marked the start of national prominence in athletics, first in basketball, and then after 1955, with the arrival of Doyt Perry, in football as well.

A seemingly natural outgrowth of intercollegiate athletics was the formation of leagues and the development of rivalries. In 1919 Bowling Green helped form the Northwestern Ohio Intercollegiate Athletic Association composed of five schools in northwest Ohio. In 1932 the growth of the athletic program led to leaving the NOIAA and joining the twenty-four school Ohio Athletic Conference. The continuance of growth caused the university a decade later to withdraw from the OAC and become independent. While that status worked well for basketball, it proved less satisfactory for all other sports. This fact helped dictate a new league affiliation which was completed in 1952 when Bowling Green was admitted to the Mid-American Conference. Closeness and league ties helped create a series of rivalries over the first fifty years, but the first and the longest standing one was with the University of Toledo. Competition between the two schools began in the 1917-1918 basketball season and grew more intense over the years until it finally overflowed. The rivalry became so aggravated that from 1935 until 1947 all athletic competition was suspended. With the entry into the Mid-American Conference a number of new rivalries emerged and have continued.[23]

"Studies come first always, but they are not the whole of a college education" stated the 1961-62 catalog.[24] Ironically commencing in 1949, this had been true of campus. Restiveness and occasional disorder checkered university life from the post-war years into the early 1960s. The strains tended to arise from the growing differential in social mores between long established university attitudes and those of the veterans and the following student generation. Among these differences were such issues as car rules, alcoholic use, rules for women that were felt to be inequitable, class attendance regulations, and a generally perceived paternalistic administrative attitude.

In 1949, 1957, and 1961 student protests occurred. While each manifested itself in somewhat different ways they all garnered attention both locally and nationally. The demonstration in 1949 made the last years of President Prout's administration somewhat dismal for him and the demonstration of 1961 helped lead to the resignation of President McDonald.[25]

The Faculty and Administration

As the many aspects of student life on campus evolved over the years, so did that of the faculty and the administration. In the early years university administration was simple—the president supervised and the faculty did much of the work. Gradually, as the school grew, specific administrative functions became full-time. Among these first positions were those of Librarian, Dean of Women, and Registrar. As noted earlier, in the first years university committees were formed, such as the Social and the Athletic Committees, which were composed of faculty as well as students. With the passage of time both student/faculty and purely faculty committees proliferated so that by 1936 there were ten of them and by 1952 twenty-four.

The first fifty years of the university witnessed a changing pattern in administrative and faculty governance. Until 1930 the president, with some consultation, made all administrative decisions. In that year President Williams created an Executive Committee composed of himself, the Deans, and the Registrar which functioned as the primary policy making body until 1951. Faculty involvement appeared in 1938 when ten faculty were added to the committee. That arrangement was ended in 1942 with the creation of a University Senate and a smaller three-person Advisory Committee. This pattern was modified in 1951 with the addition of three councils—Academic, Faculty, and Student —each of which dealt with a specific area. All of these vehicles for faculty involvement became viewed as inadequate and helped lead to the significant changes that occurred following the end of the McDonald administration.[26]

The administrative staff increased in size as the complexity of the university changed. Initially there were five administrative officers and assistants. This figure was thirteen in 1929 and thirty-two by the inauguration of President Prout. The number of officers remained steady until the latter years of the McDonald administration when a sharp rise to sixty-nine occurred. The increase in positions rather clearly reflected the growth of colleges and residence life.[27]

-Money-
Fees, Costs, and Salaries

Change, as has been seen, comes in a variety of forms—new traditions, increased enrollment, curricular growth, etc.. Another reflection was the rise in the cost of an education at Bowling Green. During the first three years there were no fees and only room and board payments—an estimated $127.50 per year plus incidentals—were necessary for a resident student. In 1917 for the first time a fee of $2.00 per semester was charged, which combined with increased costs made the total estimated expenditure for the year 1920, $142.50. As the years passed fees not only increased but began to proliferate from a single activity fee to a variety of fees.

A survey of fees over the period from 1920 to 1963 shows a steady rise in the expense of attending. In 1930 total costs were listed at $208.00 of which $58.00 were for fees. By 1940 the same figures were $242.50 and $85.00. In 1946 a new fee was assessed, that on non-residents or out of state students which was placed at $25.00 per semester. While this new charge did not seem to inhibit initially the flow of out-of-state students, in time it did have that effect. Educational costs by 1950 were $436.00 per year, $136.00 of which was in fees. This did not include an extra $75.00 for non-residents. Comparable figures for 1960 show a marked increase to $1110.00 including $360.00 in fees plus for out of state students an extra $300.00.[28]

The steady growth in the cost of education was the result of a number of factors. Among them were inflation, an increasingly larger physical plant, and increased numbers of faculty and staff. Salaries became a significant segment of the total university budget. From 1914 until the 1950s they were kept at a slow rate of growth, and by general consensus at a level below national faculty compensation. During the McDonald administration a major effort was made to upgrade both the qualifications of the faculty and their pay. General salary ranges during the first fifty years demonstrate the pattern of growth in costs.

In 1914 the salaries for the ten full time faculty ranged from $1500 to $2000 per year. By 1928 the range ran from $2400 to $4400 where it basically remained until the close of World War II. The salary range for 1949-50 had risen slightly to $2500 to $5000. The first year that President McDonald established his salary plan, 1952-53, the range was $3000 to $7000 with a considerable differential built in for the doctorate and those actively working toward one. A decade later, 1961-62, salaries ran from $4800 to $15,000. This dramatic rise in the 1950s was funded significantly by the two and one half times jump in student fees.[29]

The Campus Grows

Bowling Green State University has been expanding its plant to provide the best possible environment for university life and learning...[30]

During the first forty years the campus did not quite double in size from its original eighty-two and a half acres, if the acquisition of 120 acres for an airport is excluded. That amount of land not only met the building needs of the school, but also provided well into the 1930s "...ample space for agricultural experiments, school gardens, and nature study excursions."[31]

The changing academic needs led to a gradual increase in the number of buildings. When students first arrived on campus in the Fall of 1915 there were two academic buildings, a dormitory, and the heating plant. Fifteen years later that number stood at eight, and another decade later had risen to twelve. The decade of the 1940s witnessed a dramatic increase owing to the building of twenty-three "cottages" to house the new Greek groups and to the procurement of temporary buildings to meet the demands of the influx of veterans. Further building began in the late 1950s with the construction of dormitories and additional academic facilities. This spurt meant that by the 1963-64 academic year there were sixty-nine buildings in use.[32]

The building growth of the late 50s and early 60s entailed the acquiring of more land. As a consequence, the campus grew six fold in acreage during the years from 1954 to 1964. By the end of the administration of President Harshman the university was composed of 886 acres excluding the airport. The campus not only expanded over the first fifty years but changed substantially in its physical appearance. Board walks, dirt streets, and often muddy paths were the hallmarks of the campus for the first four years or so. By the early 1920s they had been replaced by pavement and a traffic circle in front of the Administration Building (University Hall). Late in the same decade gateways were constructed at the three main entries to the campus on Wooster, Court, and Ridge streets. That general configuration remained for the next thirty years. In 1958 a decision was made to enclose the inner campus and to make it largely a green space. The transformation occurred during the summer of 1959 with the creation of the inner campus as it appears today.[33]

A Kaleidoscope of Fifty Years

Changing patterns and growth marked the history of the first fifty years of Bowling Green. A variety of forces, some planned and others not, played a role in the evolution of a small, fledgling teacher's school into a university. While many individuals were involved in the process, and absolutely essential to its success, three men predominantly influenced the period. They were Homer B. Williams, Frank J. Prout, and Ralph W. McDonald.

Williams served as president for a little over half of the first fifty years. He did much to mold the basic nature and character of Bowling Green. He held a vision of a university emerging from the small beginnings, and gave the foresighted leadership that made that dream an organic reality by the time that he retired in 1937.

President Prout served the university during the momentous years of World War II and the post war veterans influx. Much of his time was spent in the daily demands of keeping the university functioning. In addition, however, to helping Bowling Green weather those trying times, he left a further mark. He encouraged the sound growth of both the new undergraduate colleges and placed graduate education on a sound base. He also institutionalized the national Greek system on the campus and enhanced further the involvement of students in the decision making process.

While the decade of President McDonald's administration ended in seeming disarray, he had amalgamated during his administration a university from the ingredients that his predecessors had gathered. By 1961 a firm base existed of a solid academic curriculum and organization, a qualified faculty, and a suitable physical plant. All of the necessary elements for a university of 6000 or 15,000 were present only waiting for the next twenty-five years to unfold.

Notes

Chapter I

1. Robert J. Overman, *The History of Bowling Green State University* (Bowling Green, Ohio: Bowling Green University Press, 1967), p. 14.

2. Ibid., pp. 14-15.

3. Ibid., pp. 22-24.

4. Ibid., pp. 25-30.

5. *THE BEEGEE.* Issued annually by the Students of the State Normal College, Bowling Green, Ohio, 1918. pp. 75-78. Taken from "We Hail You, Dear Normal College" writen in 1915 by Ernest Hesser, Instructor in Music.

6. Second Annual Catalogue, 1915-1916, Vol. II, Number 3, Bowling Green State Normal College, May 1916. p. 19.

7. Overman, *History,* pp. 32-36.

8. Ibid., pp. 36-39.

9. Daniel Elsbrock, et al., *History of Residence Life at Bowling Green State University* (Typed Manuscript), 1980, pp. 45-46.

10. Overman, Passim, pp. 29, 61, 80, 108, 125, 162-3, & 202.

11. Manuscript, 376, The Stuart R. Givens Collection, #14 and Overman, *History,* pp. 208-09.

12. Overman, *History,* Passim, pp. 26-7, 66-7, 83, 136-7, 141, & 169-70.

13. Annual Catalogue. Vol. II, Number 3 (1916), Vol X, Number 3 (1924), Vol. XXIII, Number 3 (1937), Vol. XXXVIII, Number 1 (1952), and Vol. XLIX, Number 2 (1963), BGSNC & BGSU, B.G., O., Passim.

14. Annual Catalogue, 1914 - pp. 49-50 & 64; 1929 - pp. 59-86; 1939 - pp. 91-153; 1952 - pp. 160-238.

15. Annual Catalogue. Second (1916) and Tenth (1924). pp. 20 and 26 and Bulletin of Bowling Green State University, Catalogue Number 1936-1937, Vol. XXIII, Number 3, May, 1937, p. 22.

16. Overman, *History,* pp. 32-33, 141-42, & 170.

17. MS-376, #10f.

18. The BEEGEE, pp. 76-77.

19. Overman, *History,* pp. 65 & 143.

20. Ibid., pp. 39, 52-54, & 92.

21. Ibid., p. 145.

22. Ibid., pp. 62-63, 72-74, 142-45, 177, & 179.

23. Ibid., pp. 53, 71-72, 93, & 180-81.

24. Bulletin, 1961-62, p. 59.

25. Overman, *History,* pp. 145-48 and 183-87.

26. Ibid., pp. 62, 82, 97, 115-17, & 171-7.

27. Bulletin - 1919 - pp. 7-16; 1929 - pp. 6 & 22-3; 1939 - pp. 4-5; 1963 - pp. 206-7.

28. Elsbrock, *Residence Life,* pp. 40-41.

29. Board of Trustees Minutes. Microfilm. Rolls 1 and 2, June 1911 to June 1950 and Overman, *History,* pp. 165-67.

30. Annual Catalogue. 1962-63, p. 5

31. Ibid., 1936-37, p. 22

32. Ibid., 1915-16, p. 20; 1930-31, pp. 18-19; 1952-3, pp. 30-33; 1963-64, pp. 5-7.

33. Overman, *History,* pp. 45, 60, and 160-61.

SECTION II
YEARS OF GROWTH

The Jerome Administration
1963-1970

William Travers Jerome III
President — 1963-1970

20

CHAPTER II

THE CAMPUS
Its Physical, Academic, and Human Dimensions

The Campus — 1963

CHAPTER II

THE CAMPUS
Its Physical, Academic, and Human Dimensions

In September 1963 William Travers Jerome III became the sixth President of the University. He arrived in Bowling Green having just turned forty-four years old, and after having spent the previous ten years as a teacher and then dean in the College of Business at Syracuse University. His educational background and experience were exclusively that of private educational institutions and included a doctorate from the Harvard Business School.

Jerome assumed the presidency at what was probably the most placid period for the university of the entire 1960s. During the previous two years the tensions and problems that erupted during the last year of President McDonald's administration had subsided. The two-year term of President Harshman had done much to ameliorate conditions and to reconcile the faculty. The future looked bright with prospects of great growth under the direction of a new, vigorous president. Outside the university the nation was experiencing the exuberance of another youthful president and the illusion of a revived Camelot. In August 1963 the spirit of the nation was buoyed by Martin Luther King, Jr. and his "dream," only to be dashed three months later in Dallas with the assassination of President Kennedy. After the initial shock the country seemed to steady under the leadership of President Johnson, but 1964 brought the Tonkin Gulf, Mario Savio, and the beginning of doubt and criticism. President Jerome, then, assumed office just before the event in Dallas led into, as one commentator saw it, a period of "paralysis, gloom, and reappraisal."[1]

A Tone and Direction

"...a center for creativity rather than just another citadel of conformity."[2]

The philosophy of the new president and the goals that he
held for the university were clearly expressed during his first
year. In his opening address to the faculty in September, 1963
entitled "The Task Ahead", Jerome called for mutual trust and
confidence and for a willingness to seek after dreams. He
challenged the faculty to help develop an atmosphere in which
great teaching and genuine scholarship could flourish in an integrated, interdisciplinary setting. Several more themes which
proved to be continuing ones throughout his administration
were set forth. Among them were the need to expose students to
foreign cultures, aesthetic values, data processing, an enhanced
freshman experience, and an increased appreciation of the
power of ideas. In the latter regard he called upon faculty to
teach students to not only be debunkers, but also to master the
"...skills required to become successful doers."[3]

A year later, September 1964, in his inaugural address President Jerome elaborated further on his educational philosophy
and his hopes for Bowling Green. The entire inaugural event
centered around the theme "The State University—Creator or
Conformist," with its stylized logo of the tree of knowledge.
Prior to his speech several notable individuals dealt with the
topic. Among them were R. Sargent Shriver, Director of the
Peace Corp, Lauris Norstad, President of Owens-Corning
Fiberglass, William R. Tolley, Chancellor, Syracuse Univer-
sity, and Anthony J. Celebrezze, Secretary of the Department of
Health, Education, and Welfare. The essence of President
Jerome's message can be seen in the following two quotations:

"...educated man must learn to become master of his machines
and of his economy rather than the servant of them. He is the
one to dictate the new technology and not vice versa. Pressures
on the state universities...to provide ever more practical training
for a world of work, can badly augment...the imbalance between society's commitment to the physical sciences and its commitment to the social sciences and humanities."

"...man now has the scientific and technological knowhow literally to control his physical environment and to invent his future. But to shape this future and to make it a joy forever, we must learn much more about man as a thinking, sentient being.

We must also discover new and more effective ways for him to govern. We must strive to break down all unnecessary barriers to communication that our highly specialized and fragmentized world of the intellect has created for us. And above all, we must continue to remind ourselves and our students that, in today's world, dreams and faith and brave fellowship still have a revered place."[4]

During the remainder of his presidency Jerome continued in speeches and in practice to apply his philosophy to the administration of the university. He argued continually that teaching at all levels needed to be improved and that the greatest need for institutional improvement lay in the area of student advising and counseling. He constantly reiterated the indispensability of creative approaches to problems. The latter included matters of academic programs, institutional governance, and contacts with society beyond the confines of the university. These ideas were most clearly seen in the opening address to the faculty in 1966 entitled "On Directions, Dreams, and Madness." He summarized his thoughts in that speech by saying "If we identify our mission and goals with wisdom and vision, and then proceed to accomplish these with dispatch, with energy, and with good will, I worry not about greatness. It will be thrust upon us."[5] The commitment of university human and other resources to the solution of social and ecological problems was a further theme which emerged more urgently as the decade ended. In the Fall of 1968 he asserted that public universities could no longer afford "...to sit on the sidelines of society and carp," for if they did leadership would be lost to "...demigods and the mob."[6]

At times image, as well as substance, emerged as policy. Late in the Summer of 1965 an official university publication appeared under the title of the *Bowling Green University Magazine*. This was the beginning of an effort by President Jerome to drop the word state from all but the most official of university documents. He asserted that the full name was both "too ponderous" and parochial and did not convey the new life and direction that he held for the university. While the idea was never adopted a reminder of it still exists on the I-75 road signs constructed at the time which read Bowling Green University.[7]

The Campus Grows

The seven years of the Jerome administration were very prolific years for building construction at the university. All told some fifteen buildings and several special facilities were planned and built. The period was also marked by an increased emphasis on campus planning, resulting partially from the president's awareness of enrollment pressures, and partially from the mandate of the newly formed Ohio Board of Regents for priority listings of capital improvements. These pressures led Jerome during the Fall of 1963 to initiate actions on short and long range planning. A first step was approval by the Board of Trustees of top priority for a new library and the development of a science complex. Simultaneously, he formed the Campus Beautification Committee, quickly dubbed the Beautniks, in order to oversee the aesthethic development of the campus including its landscaping. The final early initiative was to engage the consulting firm of Caudill, Rowlett, and Scott (CRS) of Houston to assist in the long range planning process.

CRS was asked to suggest a campus configuration for enrollments projected at 15,000 and at 30,000. During a period of over two years a great deal of discussing, suggesting, rejecting, and redrafting occurred before the final report was submitted in the Fall of 1966. In its opening analysis the report (belaboring the obvious) stated that "Although the Bowling Green area is not heavily endowed with such naturally attractive features as mountains, streams, and forests, the countryside is nevertheless blessed with prosperous farms and rich green vegetation."[8] Much of the report dealt with enhancing the attractiveness of the campus. To accomplish that end CRS proposed the closing of the inner campus area to vehicular traffic and the creation of more open space. That concept dictated the recommendation that Ridge Street east of Thurstin be closed

including the drive into the Union Oval. Openness and access to
the Union would be provided by the demolition of sorority row
and Shatzel and Johnston Halls. A similar opening and access
would be developed for the new library by the removal of the
old fraternity row. To compensate for the loss of fraternity and
sorority housing a fifteen acre area at the east end of the airport
was suggested.

Based on information from the preliminary state master plan
the report assumed a student mix of approximately thirty-five
percent lower division, fifty percent upper division, and fifteen
percent graduate level. The smaller lower division enrollment
elicited the most unusual and controversial part of the plan; the
proposed creation of discrete residential colleges of 700 students
each in which living, learning, and recreation would be
centered. At the 15,000 level the college units would be located
west of Yount Road between Ridge Street and Poe Road, and at
the 30,000 level additional units would be placed along the east
side of North College Drive. At 30,000 then the campus was
designed like a doughnut with Oak Grove Cemetery as the hole.
To handle the expected increase in graduate housing needs an
area of seventy five acres outside of the main campus was provided east of Mercer Road and north of Poe Road.

With the establishment in 1963 of the Ohio Board of Regents
capital improvements priority listings from each university were
mandated with each listing projected over three bienniums. The
listings which were submitted every two years give a good picture of the plans, dreams, and directions for growth that were
held during the sixties, and beyond. The priorities given
reflected in part, at least, a dream list with the number of
buildings and the monetary requests well above the level approved by the state. This can clearly be seen by listing facilities
that appeared during the Jerome years but were never funded.
They included: a Continuing Education Center, Performing
Arts Center, Child Study Center, new Health and Physical
Education Complex, Language Building, Instructional Media
Center, Social Sciences Building, Field House, addition to
Memorial Hall, and parking garages.

Despite the preceding list, a number of buildings were planned, initiated, and/or completed between 1963 and 1970. Of
those buildings approximately half were state financed and half

were funded by bonds sold by the university. The state granted money only for structures that were clearly academic in nature such as the Library, Life Sciences, Mathematical Sciences, Psychology, Education, and Business Administration. The many auxiliary buildings essential to a residential campus were financed with bonds. These included Harshman, Kreischer, and Offenhauer residence halls, the Student Services Building, the Student Health Center, and the Ice Arena. Included in the long range plans and bonded building during this period was the development of intercollegiate sports facilities east of Yount Road. This led to the construction of the Stadium, baseball diamond, all-weather track, nine hole golf course, a number of playing and practice fields, including ones for intramural activities, and satellite parking areas.

The marked increase in construction raised a number of questions such as the sitings for new buildings and the naming of them. Once the long range plan was developed the siting issue was largely settled, but in early years of building that was not the case. In the original planning the new science complex was to be east of Oak Grove Cemetery and Williams Hall was considered as a location for the new library. The question of names was resolved by the Board of Trustees when in May 1966 it adopted a policy statement on the matter. The policy provided that:

1. Academic buildings would be named for their function or purpose. Exceptions to this could occur when a significant donation was made to the construction or maintance of a building. Special rooms and facilities within buildings could be designated for particular faculty, administrators, individuals, and companies.

2. Residence halls would carry the names of persons who have contributed significantly in terms of service to the university.

3. Normally names would not be given to structures while an individual was alive.[9] (The third proviso has been honored in the breach.)

Other issues that emerged from the building program were those of providing for adequate parking and the paying for such lots, dealing with the government in planning and campus expansion, developing various special facilities, assuring an aesthetic campus environment and the financing for it, and deciding on future housing. Once the total university community began to increase on a steady basis parking became a permanent problem. Parking lots were built with the inner ones being for faculty and staff and the outer ones for commuter and residential students. When initially students were charged a fee to help finance the building and maintenance but faculty and staff were not complaints arose. Criticism was also aired over the underutilization of faculty lots. By the Fall of 1966 the situation was such that the *BG News* editorially asserted that the students were being treated as "third class citizens," and a letter to the editor asked why the faculty should have privileged parking since they were really employees of the students. A member of the English Department replied that "The answer is simple. Servants are hard to find these days."[10] Periodically from that time on questions were raised about parking. In the Fall of 1969 it was announced that a parking fee would be assessed on the faculty and staff. When a number objected stating that parking was a fringe benefit the plan was revised by deducting the charges from departmental and area operating budgets.

Government, both federal and state, played an increased role in building. The Federal Higher Education Facilities Act of 1963 provided the university with several million dollars to help with the construction of the science complex, the library and the College of Education building. Along with governmental support came involvement in the planning process. While that was neither new or unexpected it was, at times, annoying. Two examples of this occurred in 1966 and 1967. Early in 1966 the Improvements Inspection Committee of the state legislature questioned the plans for the Student Services Building on the grounds of style —more expensive— and the type of financing —student fees. These objections were surmounted and the building eventually was given a national architectural award. In the middle of 1967 the State Architect informed the university that the Ohio Board of Regents had reservations about the large lecture halls, the "excessively" wide halls, and the round exterior stairwells of the proposed mathematical sciences building. An issue again resolved favorably by the university.[11]

The continued planning for improvements by the university, the state, and the city necessitated cooperation even though difficult at times. One of the last links in the building of Interstate 75 was the Bowling Green bypass. When the decision to run it east of Bowling Green was reached university property was involved. Negotiations ran over several months as the administration attempted to reach a favorable settlement. In September 1967 a contract was signed whereby the state agreed to light the exit area on Wooster, construct a chain fence along the west side of the road, provide a utility tunnel under the highway, and pay the university $235,000 for the 14.91 acres of land used for the right of way.[12] Much of 1967 was consumed with discussion between the city and the university made essential by the actual or the anticipated growth of both. A comprehensive agreement was reached late in the year dealing with sewer lines, the exchange of property, the closing of streets, and improvement of other streets. While a number of these arrangements did not transpire, some did such as the aligning of the entrance of Parking Lot A with South College, the improvement of both Thurstin Street and Yount Road from Wooster Street north, and the transfer of land that led in time to the relocation of the city sewage treatment plant.[13]

An integral element of a major university is its specialized facilities, and entering the 1960's Bowling Green had few of these. During the decade a number of them evolved or were seriously considered. While a television band had been reserved for BGSU in 1953, an application to broadcast was not made to the Federal Communications Commission until June, 1963. Approval for a 1000 watt transmitter was granted and on February 10, 1964 the first telecast was aired from studios in South Hall. Once regular broadcasting commenced it was clear that the physical facilities were inadequate. Consequently, a H.E.W. grant was successfully sought which afforded the university the opportunity to construct a separate studio off Clough Street on the south campus. This structure opened in 1967 and has remained the center for WBGU-TV.[14] Two other electronic additions of the decade sprang from the need for better computer and telephone capabilities. In 1962 the university acquired its first centrally controlled computer which was geared at servicing primarily academic and research purposes. The center created, it employed a half-time director and a half-time secretary. In 1965 the system was enhanced in order to handle administrative demands as well. During the rest of the 60s the operation expanded so that by the end of the decade an operation known as Computational Services had emerged with a director and a staff of twenty - nine full-time and twelve part-time individuals.[15] The significant increase in the size of both the faculty and the residential student population outdistanced the ability of the local telephone company to maintain service. Therefore, the decision was made in early 1967 to install a centrex system that could serve the total university much more efficiently even though at greater cost. The plan was implemented and became operative in 1969. The main equipment was housed in the original heating plant which had become the Maintenance Building. In May 1969 the name was changed to the Centrex Building.[16]

A number of other facilities reflecting the increased research and residential emphasis of the university mushroomed. These ranged from an animal research building and a greenhouse, to such student oriented structures as the ice arena, all-weather track, and a health center. Another important addition to Bowling Green, which occurred largely unknown to the main campus student body, was the development of the Firelands Campus in Huron. From 1956 onward Bowling Green had operated a branch at the Sandusky High School. By the middle of the 1960s the citizens of Erie, Huron, and Ottawa counties wanted a permanent, independent branch. In order to get state funding a major fund campaign, headed by Theodore Wakefield of Huron, was launched in the tri-county area and was oversubscribed. Consequently, by the late 60s a new branch campus had been created in Huron.[17]

During 1963 and into early 1964 it seemed that another campus might be acquired. The United States Army as an economy move decided to close the Rossford Ordinance Depot and dispose of the land. The University with encouragement from the newly formed Board of Regents, seriously considered acquiring part of it for use as a technical college site. President Jerome early in his presidency questioned the need and the university withdrew from involvement in what did become Owens Technical College.[18]

As indicated earlier a major concern of President Jerome was the appearance and aesthetic development of the campus. Much effort, time, and money was expended in accomplishing that end. The concern manifested itself in both the exterior and interior appearance of buildings, general landscaping, and the use of art. A decision was made early that while a uniformity of architectural style would not be attempted, a conformity to materials—brick and glass or cement and glass—would be maintained.[19] Landscaping of buildings and of the whole campus area was a priority item. In early 1965 the Director of Institutional Planning in a memo suggested to Vice President Ervin J. Kreischer that the cost of the total site development be included in the cost estimates for new structures. He enquired if he wanted to discuss it, to which Jerome on his carbon copy replied across the bottom in red "Discuss, hell! Make sure all projects have provision of $ for appropriate landscaping. MAKE SURE this is on your programming CHECKLIST."[20] As construction occurred improvements in the general topography resulted in the creation of two ponds and the creation of a hill at the east end of the campus. The pond along Yount Road was named Peregrine Pond and the hill was quickly dubbed Bill's Hill or Mount Jerome. All of these efforts emphasized the extensive planting of trees and shrubs, and were coordinated by a landscape designer employed specifically for that task.[21]

One other important form of enhancing the beauty of the campus was the use of decorative art. An artist in residence*, Donald Drumm, was commissioned to create a number of works. His most apparent and controversial one was the murals and sculpture placed on the exterior of the new library. Many of the new buildings had interior murals for the entry areas or had some unique architectural design built in. A different approach was the placement in many administrative offices of paintings and pieces of art created by students and faculty and paid for from the Jerome family connected Hope Colgate Sloane Fund.[22] Exterior visual effects were created with a fountain in

* President Jerome once described an Artist in Residence "As a person who is never here when you want them."

front of the Administration Building and Drumm's 1970 statue entitled "A Bridge Over Troubled Waters" near the Commons. One effort went awry for over a decade. In 1965 the university purchased for $35,000 twelve fragmentary panels from a Second Century A.D. floor mosaic from the ancient city of Antioch. The intent was to incorporate them into the new library, but that did not materialize. Consequently, they were stored for over ten years before they were placed in the hallway of the renovated McFall Center.[23]

While construction was extensive during the Jerome administration, only one residence hall was planned and completed. The reasons for this were many. In the first years of his administration President Jerome found that the dormitories planned and/or built under President McDonald were almost sufficient. One further hall (Kreischer Quadrangle) was felt necessary and that was authorized by the Board of Trustees in November, 1965. For the next four years discussions and on again/off again decisions occurred concerning the need and the type of housing that should be approved. Initially two major factors influenced the debate. One centered around the residential college concept put forth in the Caudill, Rowlett, and Scott long range planning proposal. The other was the Board of Regents and its first Master Plan which proposed a rearrangement of the student mix at the university level with an increased emphasis on upper-level and graduate enrollments. By early 1967 the time seemed to have arrived to start planning another facility. However, in September the Board, following a recommendation of the administrative heads responsible for finances and planning, agreed to halt the project. The reasons given were: increased costs over the original estimates; the uncertainty of the student mix; concern over the impact of conversion to the Quarter System; and, changing student attitudes about on-campus living. By 1969 enrollment pressures alleviated much of the doubt and led to the authorization in May to restart planning. Final financing for what was referred to as an addition to McDonald Quadrangle was approved in January, 1970. The building named after former president Roy E. Offenhauer was completed during Hollis A. Moore's first year as president.[24]

During the latter years of the Jerome administration much discussion centered around the idea of encouraging or even contracting with private builders to construct and operate dormitories and/or apartments. Several schools including Ohio University made such a decision, but despite study the university fortunately did not move quickly. In 1970 the Board of Regents acting on a legislative mandate placed an enrollment ceiling on the five residential universities thus ending largely for Bowling Green, the need for more beds.[25]

Governance

"If we can but work together with trust and confidence, I know that we will make an already good university a great one."[26]

The beginning of the Jerome administration coincided with the adoption by the Board of Trustees of the Faculty Charter. The Charter was the product of a Faculty Study Committee which had developed it over two years. It reflected clearly the desire of faculty to have a greater voice in university governance in general and a sizeable one in academic and professional matters. The Charter created a self standing, representative Faculty Senate which was to speak for the faculty and to counsel the President. The document gave considerable influence to the faculty and, therefore, was viewed variously from the President down as an asset and a liability.[27]

Administratively President Jerome did not initiate many major changes in either personnel or structure. There were four top administrators, Paul F. Leedy - Provost, Kenneth H. McFall - Vice President, Ervin J. Kreischer - Treasurer and Business Manager, and Donnal V. Smith - Dean of Students holding office in September, 1963, and those same four offices with slight name changes still existed when Jerome resigned in 1970. In the interim three of the four (Leedy, Kreischer, and Smith) were replaced because they had reached mandatory retirement age. The three replacements who served into the Moore years were: Stanley K. Coffman - Vice President for Academic Affairs and Dean of Faculties, Bobby D. Owens - Vice President for Research and Financial Affairs, and James G. Bond - Vice President for Student Affairs; all of whom were internal appointments.

While the organization and the people running it did not change appreciably, a new administrative style and emphasis did emerge. The management approach—one of delegation—was reflected by Provost Leedy at the end of President Jerome's first year when he wrote "You as President have delegated more authority to me as Provost than the office has ever had before..."[28] This view continued to be the dominant one throughout the duration of Jerome's presidency. An increased emphasis in several directions also became a hallmark of the administration. Two offices, both of which dealt with longer range concerns, were created. In 1964 the Office of Development was formed with Charles E. Perry named its first Director. This initiated a permanent ongoing program of external fund raising. The following year, 1965, an Office of Institutional Research and Planning under Donald C. Lelong was created. The President gave as the rationale for its being that it would enable the university to know better what it was doing and what can be done better. In 1967 the title was changed to Office of Institutional Studies and Planning.[29]

A major ingredient in the developmental planning process was another innovation of the President—Key Result Areas (KRA). The scheme entailed each unit of the university submitting annually an organized list of its accomplishments and goals. This process on an individual and composite basis was aimed at taking the pulse of the university and getting a feel for things to be done. The eventual end was expressed by President Jerome in a memorandum to the Board of Trustees when he stated that "This suggests further that the success achieved in these areas is ultimately a way of measuring the competence of the President...happy thought that this is!"[30]

While Jerome was intrigued with "Directions, Dreams, and Madness" as expounded in his 1966 speech to the faculty, he like any other university president realized that the heart of the institution was its academic vitality and fiscal integrity. To these matters let us turn.

The Atmosphere

"We can not give you (wisdom) — no matter how hard we try. We can only provide the environment which will make your own search a rich and satisfying one."[31]

The seven years of the Jerome administration were ones in which he, the faculty, and the students carried on a dialogue over the academic purposes of the university, and about how they might best be attained. The culmination of this process was the creation in 1969 of the Commission on the Mission of the University whose report, not surprisingly, was not universally accepted. Much of the difficulty in reaching a consensus was centered in the radicalization of student thinking as the decade of the 1960's unfolded. This development resulted often in confusion, indecision, and strife which divided internally both the faculty and the student body, and pitted the various elements against one another. In spite of these issues many changes did occur in academic programs, degree offerings, academic organization, academic delivery systems, and the quality of the students and faculty.

The Academic Objectives

For a twenty year period, 1957-1977, the *Bulletin* (catalogue) of the university carried on its first page a general statement of academic purpose, the context of which was little changed. However, around that statement a whirlwind of debate swirled. The central figure was the President who addressed academic issues and philosophy in all of his Fall speeches to the faculty. In those presentations he ranged the gamut from aesthetic values to solving the problems of society and the environment, although he centered heavily on effective teaching. Several factors helped focus discussion, but by their nature opened questions of emphasis.

The Faculty Charter and later the first Master Plan of the Board of Regents both stated that the goal of the university was to teach, do research, and perform public service. Much debate raged around whether these were of equal value, and, if not, what was the order of importance. This issue was made more acute by the rapid growth of graduate education which accentuated the possible dichotomy between teaching and research. As 1970 approached one other major element arose - the demand of students for "relevance" and a greater role in establishing goals and setting curriculum. This last development along with the over-all discussion on academic goals was part of a general national debate on the directions — even survival — of higher education in the United States.[32]

During the Jerome administration two different ad hoc groups were commissioned to study and make recommendations on academic aims. The first of these, the Committee on Long-Range Planning for Faculty Personnel, established by the President in November, 1964, placed considerable weight on research and upper level and graduate teaching. Two years later, a Commission to Study the Mission of the University chaired by Robert P. Goodwin in a report commonly called "The White Paper," reflected the change in circumstances since the earlier report. It called for a greater stress on teaching values, increased involvement of students in all areas of policy making, more attention to under graduate education, and democratization of the student-faculty relationship.[33]

President Jerome had asserted that the activity of the Commission was one of the most important in the history of the university. Consequently, "The White Paper" was viewed by the university community seriously. While there was much support for the report a number of objections were raised to its seeming catering to student demands, its ignoring of the unique nature of a residential campus, and its lack of concern with alumni, the community, parents, or the region.[34] During the academic year 1969-70 various student groups, the Faculty Senate, the Academic Council, the Alumni Board, and the Board of Trustees read and discussed the report. Since its basic recommendations lay within the purview of the Academic Council that body was looked to for the development of a policy statement that reflected the essence of the year long debate. On May 13, 1970 Academic Council adopted a statement entitled "The Mission of the University" which called for a balance between under, upper, and graduate education and teaching, research, and service. A plea was also made for more innovative approaches to teaching, and a university-wide acceptance of the value of broad-based, liberal education for all students.[35]

Academic Growth
- By Conversion, Degrees, and Other Means -

Even while the debate on academic philosophy and policy was proceeding major educational influences significantly affected the university. Two of these of importance in the latter 1960s were the Master Plan of 1965 and the OBOR decision to convert all higher educational institutions to the quarter system.

In the Spring of 1965 the Regents released its first Master Plan which proposed an enrollment limit of 15,000 Full Time Equivalent students with an emphasis on upper level and graduate education. That plan coupled with the general national trend toward greater graduate and professional offerings led to a marked increase in degrees offered and programs instituted or planned. In 1963 twelve degrees, six at the baccalaureate level and six at the graduate level, were available while by 1971 the figure stood at eighteen with one Associate, eight Baccalaureate, and nine graduate degrees offered. Another reflection of the growth was that twelve disciplines began awarding master's degrees for the first time during that period as well as four additional ones at the Ph.D. level. By 1969 the Board of Trustees had also authorized the planning and phasing in of five more doctoral programs, and possibly two additional cooperative ones, for a total of twelve.[36]

"Your decision relative to the comon calendar is not 'planning' but administration by executive fiat."[37] Such was the response of President Jerome to Chancellor John Millett's announcement in September 1966 of a proposed conversion of all state universities within a year to the quarter calendar. The retort which had considerable faculty support was more critical of the Chancellor's handling of the matter than of the plan itself. A vigorous debate involving the faculty and administration ran throughout the month of October. In both a general faculty meeting and the Faculty Senate the Chancellor was attacked for exceeding the authority of the Regents and for using budgetary means as a way of coercing cooperation. By late October Millett indicated that he had not intended to mandate conversion by the Fall of 1967. With that concession Jerome recommended that serious consideration be given to the quarter system solely on its merits. Based on a study begun early in the

Fall the Faculty Senate at its November meeting recommended the adoption of a Quarter Calendar commencing in September 1968. On December 7th in a referendum vote the student body affirmed the position which a week later was approved officially by the Board of Trustees. Thus, for the next fourteen years the university functioned on the Quarter System.[38]

While the university succumbed to uniformity on the calendar issue, in many areas diversity and innovation flourished. Among the manifestation of this was the emergence of several academically oriented specialized centers such as the Drosophila Center, the Center for Research in Social Behavior, the Philosophy Documentation Center, The Anderson Center, the Northwest Ohio-Great Lakes Research Center, and the Center for the Study of Popular Culture. In the purely academic realm for the first time bachelor degrees were offered in the specialized areas of music and technology and an associate degree in applied business. Also international education grew. In 1963 there was an International Studies Program, but little else. By 1970 there were evolving area study programs in Asia, Latin America, Eastern Europe and the Soviet Union, and international business plus Academic Centers located in Madrid, Tours, and Salzburg. On campus the first director for international students was appointed with a subsequent increase of countries represented from fourteen to fifty. One other dimension of the growing multiethnicity of Bowling Green was the initiation of an Upward Bound Program in 1966 and the beginnings in 1969 of a Student Development Program.[39]

Delivering the Academic Product

The goal of creating a more effective academic organization and an improved means of transmitting knowledge was a desire, if not an actual necessity, of the growth years of the Jerome era. In many of his speeches President Jerome called for changes that would provide better educational service. An ever improving academic climate was needed and could occur if effective, innovative teaching were fostered. While better teaching was essential, other factors were also necessary, such as improved buildings and equipment, the use of the latest electronic techniques, more interdisciplinary studies, and new organizational approaches.[40]

From the beginning of the Jerome administration many proposals, much discussion, considerable planning, and some actual new organizational approaches occurred. The CRS Study
at both the fifteen and thirty thousand enrollment levels was
predicated on the concept of residential colleges. That idea was
discussed at great length over a three year period as a primary
means of enriching the freshman experience through closer contact within a learning community of students and faculty. The
climax of this proposal was reached in the Fall of 1967 when a
four-day conference was held entitled "Improving the University Climate for Higher Learning: Experimental and Residential
Colleges."[41] In time as residence hall building ended with the
enrollment cap the residential college concept faded, only to
emerge over a decade later in the discrepant form of an honors'
dorm. Another idea promoted by the administration was the
university or general college model in which some or many first
and second year students would be enrolled. There were a
number of variants suggested running from a one or two year
experience for undecided students to a mandatory associate of
arts degree program. Again nothing came of the notion for a
decade, when it too resurfaced as the University Division of the
College of Arts and Sciences.[42] It is clear that a conviction persisted which was expressed clearly in the Fall of 1969 by James
G. Bond, Vice President for Student Affairs, when he told the
Board that "It is important, if we are to achieve more than
simply being in the hotel business, to provide dynamic living
and learning situations with a wide number of options."[43] This
push helped to bring approval by the following Spring of the
Little College which began functioning at the start of the Moore
administration.[44]

In March, 1967 the "Report of the Committee on Long-
Range Planning for Faculty Personnel" was submitted to the
Trustees. It accentuated the dichotomy between an emphasis on
undergraduate teaching and the development of a graduate,
research oriented faculty. The committee projected what the
ideal size faculty for 15,000 students should be and its recommendations on the mix of faculty in the years 1975 and 1990. It
suggested a faculty of 1100 (1985 figure - 700 plus) with a heavy
use of teaching fellows and predoctoral instructors for lower

level courses. The full-time tenured faculty load was to be shifted over the period increasingly to research so that by 1990 three-fourths of that group would devote one-half or more of its time to that endeavor. As with the other reorganizational proposals this one too reflected a genuine academic conviction.[45]

While much of the debate and planning aimed at improving the academic environment proved fruitless, a great many developments did help attain that end. Among them were organizational changes, new or improved methods of providing educational services, a revised Academic Honesty Code, and the at times controversial instituting of more flexible rules or requirements. During the years 1965-1967 several new departments or discipline areas were formed. The Department of Education was divided in 1965 into the six divisions of Educational Media, Student Teaching, Reading, Curriculum and Instruction, Administration and Supervision, and Foundations and Inquiry. Two years later the College of Business reorganized as follows: Continuing Departments — Business Education, Economics, Journalism, and Marketing which had been created in 1965; New Departments — Business Law, Finance and Insurance, Management, and Qualitative Analysis and Control. Two departments were redirected as well. In 1966 Geography was transfered from the College of Business to the College of Liberal Arts and the following year the Department of Art was made a School. In 1969 one other new entity was formed when the Department of Computer Science was formed.[46]

Enhancement of the many means and systems by which education was conveyed is an ongoing aspect of any university. The most important example of this in the Jerome presidency was the construction of a new library. Opened in 1967, the library while planned to meet the growing needs of the university also helped by its imposing nature to create an aura for learning. There were additionally a number of developments centered on student learning. In 1963 Martha Gesling Weber offered the first closed circuit television class — Developmental Psychology—geared at using some of the latest electronic techniques. Quite opposite from this mass approach was the introduction in 1964 of an honors program originally enrolling twenty four students. Both of these approaches were intended to improve the quality of education. To that same end the Faculty Senate in 1966 circulated to the faculty a revised "Statement on Effective Teaching" which it was hoped would help them do a better job. Another major move to serve students better was the revision of the curriculum of the College of Business implemented in the Fall of 1969. It placed much more emphasis on quantitative subjects such as mathematics, statistics, and computer science.[47]

One topic upon which students and faculty agreed was the need for a better code dealing with academic honesty. A concern raised about cheating by Student Council in the Fall of 1964 led the then forming Faculty Senate to study the question. After considerable debate the Senate passed and the President approved an Academic Honesty Code in the Spring of 1966. The general reaction was supportive.[48]

The latter 1960s witnessed a growing student restlessness with regulations and requirements; a concern with which many faculty and administrators had some sympathy. The result was debate, concession, confrontation, and refusal all of which accelerated as the decade wore on. In several areas an easing of rules helped give what President Jerome labeled "creativity to an academic climate..."[49] These changes included: moving from a limited to an unlimited class cut policy for Juniors and Seniors; eliminating the five dollar fine for classes missed the day before or after a holiday; initiating in 1967 an experiment allowing upper-class students the option of taking one class per semester on a Pass/Fail basis;[50] and introducing in 1969 an Experimental Studies Program the aim of which was "...personal growth through meaningful learning..."[51] All of these modifications tended to be compromises between an even more liberal view held by many students and some faculty and a more conservative one harbored by a portion of the faculty. One issue, the role of final examinations, was never fully resolved, and remained a divisive issue through the 1970s and into the 80s. The differences were clearly identified in late 1966 and in the Spring of 1970 by Provosts Leedy and Coffman. In December 1966 Leedy issued a statement calling for the giving of finals during the appropriate time period in Finals' Week, while Coffman supported a proposal to eliminate a formal finals period with the statement that "Exam week is sort of a farce..."[52]

Another means of improving the academic delivery system that gained great popularity among the students was the use of teacher evaluations. While the concept was far from new it did gather considerable support nationally and at Bowling Green late in the 1960s.[53] In October 1969 the Student Council with the support of Vice President Coffman and Joseph Balogh, Chair of the Faculty Senate, voted to develop a professor/course evaluation form. A month later the College of Business agreed to use student evaluations, but into the following Spring the other two colleges had not followed suit even though there was support from a number of academic administrators. The issues remained a contentious one as Hollis Moore assumed the presidency.[54]

The Student Ingredient

The years of the Jerome presidency were ones in which the student body continued to grow at an even faster pace than during the late fifties. When President Jerome assumed office in the Fall of 1963 there were 8238 students enrolled for the year, 7700 of which were undergraduates. When he left in the Spring of 1970 the student body stood at 13,782, some 12,350 of whom were undergraduates. During the entire period the relative positions of the three undergraduate colleges and the graduate program remained constant. The College of Education continued, as it had historically, to be the largest with fifty five percent of the undergraduate enrollment in 1963 and fifty three percent in 1970. As graduate enrollment increased Education dropped from fifty one and a half percent of the total student count to forty seven percent. Of the other two undergraduate colleges Liberal Arts remained second in size and actually doubled its lead over the College of Business between 1963 and 1970—a fact felt by many to be reflective of the growing anti-establishment feelings of the late sixties. Interestingly, however, because of the percentage decrease in Education and the increase of the Graduate School from seven to ten and a half percent of the total count, the relative percentage positions of the other two colleges to the total remained constant at twenty five and seventeen percent respectively.

A profile of the student body showed both constancy and change. The sex ratio remained steady with an approximately five percent difference favoring males over females. Likewise, out-of-state enrollments remained equable at approximately ten percent with Michigan, New Jersey, New York, and Pennsylvania as the leaders. In-state students continued to come from most of the eighty-eight counties with Cuyahoga County remaining number one followed by Lucas, Wood, Montgomery, and Franklin Counties. With the availability starting in 1965 of federal funds an effort toward minority recruiting was launched. The first Upward Bound students came to the campus in that year which led subsequently to a slow rise in the number of minority students by 1970.[55]

The use of the American College Test (ACT) as an admission tool was initiated with the Freshman Class of 1965. This step was part of a developing strategy for handling the increasing demand for admission within the framework of a state open admissions' policy and the OBOR imposed enrollment cap. The policy was enunciated clearly in 1966 as being composed of four parts—the high school record, class rank, personal recommendations, and the ACT score. Based upon the dormitory space available those with the highest qualifications would be admitted in the Fall with all others being offered Summer and potential Second Semester admission or Fall enrollment at a Branch Campus with subsequent transfer. A result of the enrollment pressures and the above technique was that seventy-one percent of the entering freshmen had ACT Composite Scores above the national average and eighty-nine percent of them came from the upper half of their high school classes.[56]

A theoretical consequence of the more selective policy of admission should have been a rising grade point average over the years of the late sixties. Such actually did occur with the all-university grade point average increasing from 2.45 in 1963 to 2.69 in 1970. Unfortunately, the causal relationship is not clear since grade inflation became a national trend during the same period. A further probable outcome of the new policy was an increase in the Freshman retention rate.

One final obvious upshot of the growth of the student body and the increased academic offerings mentioned earlier was the meteoric rise in degrees granted. During the commencements over which President Jerome presided a total of 16,244 diplomas were awarded which in total was only 1625 fewer than all of those given prior to 1963. While the great bulk of the degrees were at the baccalaureate level the most marked increase was at the graduate level. During the period some 2600 Master, Specialist, and Doctoral diplomas were bestowed which amounted to approximately 500 more than had been awarded in the previous fifty years. All of this meant that during the Jerome years the total number of alumni doubled.[57]

The Faculty Component

"...teacher-scholars...are by nature, training, and experience individualists."[58]

In his opening address to the faculty in September 1963 President Jerome included that statement from the recently completed Faculty Study Report. He proceeded over the next seven years to increase that breed by two and a half times. When he was appointed president there were 274 faculty members and by the time he retired the number under contract had reached 695. While there was a relationship between the increase in enrollment and the growth of the faculty the ratio was not exact. In 1963 the student-faculty ratio stood at 27.4 to 1 whereas by 1970 it had dropped to 18 to 1, while simultaneously faculty contact hours had declined somewhat.[59]

As noted earlier a debate over teaching versus research permeated the period. While teaching remained the primary concern an increased emphasis on scholarship appeared, emanating largely from the faculty. A series of developments reflected the change starting with the recommendation of the Faculty Senate in November 1963 to form a standing university committee on Faculty Leaves and Research, which was done. This step triggered the internal funding of research and augmented efforts in obtaining external grants. Consequently, more money gave more faculty support for their research. The figures ran at $50,000 on average annually internally and from $861,000 in 1965 to $1,715,000 in 1970 externally. The increased support which again fit a national pattern led President Jerome in the Fall of 1967 to assert that the teacher-researcher was the new elite of universities. In recognition of this he announced that he had just appointed the first full-time Director of Research Services whose function would be to coordinate and aid the efforts of faculty in research. Not coincidentally these occurrences paralleled the evolution of doctoral programs which in turn led to the appointment of a new type of faculty member—the research professor. In 1964 the first of these was named, John Paul Scott, an eminent psychologist. A further denoting of this was the creation in 1970 by the Board of Trustees of the University Professorship which was to recognize faculty distinguished for their scholarship. While the faculty appreciated the significance of financial support they realized that released time was of equivalent value. Evidence of this was clear with the call by the Faculty Senate for a committee on both research and leaves. In 1964 the Senate recommended to the President that a sabbatical leave program be instituted. Jerome averred his support, but declared that such a program had to be funded internally which was not then feasible. The concept endured, however, and in February 1968 the Trustees approved such a program although it was not funded until the Spring following Jerome's resignation.[60]

By the end of his administration President Jerome had presided over an appreciably enhanced faculty both in size and scholarly proclivities.

The Money Labyrinth

A substantially increasing student body and faculty and a burgeoning physical plant gave the appearance of an ever increasing flow of money. When viewed from the late 1970s the Jerome years seemed financially fortunate ones. While there was much substance to the appearance, it was partially deceiving. Total income for the period grew from $27.3 million in 1964 to almost $40 million in 1970 plus an additional $18.5 in bond revenue. This growth was significant but uneven, and at an increasing cost to the student and his family.

Two problems particularly confronted the university—those of the fluctuations in state appropriations and a substantial rise in costs. From 1963 into the 1980's only in the fiscal years 1968 and 1969 were there actual decreases in the amount awarded by the state to the university. These cuts led to an almost three-year steady state budget. Simultaneously costs were multiplying. The number of employees—staff and faculty—increased by approximately one thousand as the size of the student body and the number of buildings multiplied. Not only were more individuals being paid, but salaries were increasing with the average faculty salary rising from $9920 in 1963 to $13,115 in 1970. Other enlarged demands were for computers, markedly upward moving utility rates, ever growing bonded indebtedness, and expanding fringe benefit packages. These circumstances led President Jerome to warn of deficits during each of his last three years, and caused Vice President B.D. Owens to predict that the problem would continue through the 1970s.[61]

When the appropriations from the state were inadequate the university had several options available; retrenchment, slower growth, higher fees and charges, and increased outside support. All of those tacks were pursued. In 1968 and 1969 freezes on hiring and purchases were instituted as was a lapsing of unencumbered money. The raising of fees and charges was the primary method used. Even this rather traditional and direct solution was fraught with tension. During the late 1960s Bowling Green and the other state universities struggled with Governor James Rhodes and the fledgling Board of Regents over issues of autonomy including fees. In general the universities were able to maintain control of their fees with the consequence that between 1963 and 1970 fees rose from $400 to $711 for the year and room and board from $700 to $1005 for a total ascent from $1100 to $1716. Coupled with this was a $500 a year increase for out of state students, the state subsidy for which was terminated in 1970.[62] A greatly augmented effort was undertaken to generate income from various external sources—alumni, friends, foundations, and various federal and state agencies. In the Fall of 1964 a constitution for the Alumni Association was approved that made it basically independent of the university. From that point the organization began diligently to raise money for Bowling Green. During the next six years annual total alumni giving increased from $19,330 to $89,199, although the percentage giving remained at one fifth of the total alumni. The accumulated result by 1970 was $283,436 which while not large was an important step toward increased contact and commitment from former students. The major fund raising approach began in January 1964 when President Jerome created an Office of Development with Charles E. Perry as director. Through that office a number of new overtures ensued, several of which only developed slowly. In 1964 three enduring groups were formed—the Parents Club, the President's Club, and the Falcon Club. Planning also began for a major fund raising campaign which was officially launched in the Fall of 1966 as "Bowling Green's Mission: Expanding Horizons." An eight year goal of $10 million was announced with the first two million to be attained by 1970. By January 1970 $2.5 million had been raised in cash, pledges, gifts in kind, and charitable trust arrangements. Just as Jerome retired two other developments occurred. The Class of 1970 initiated the idea of the Senior Challenge gift and Paul Wurzburger of Cleveland donated funds that would permit the establishment of a French House on campus. One other source of income was from federal/state sources. These monies were granted to support a variety of activities including support for institutes, workshops, students, acquisition of equipment, and research. By 1970 these grants had risen from $1 million to $1.7 million. The entire sum of the efforts from outside sources during the Jerome years amounted to $3 million which while not enormous still helped lessen some of the financial strain.[63]

Notes

Chapter II

1. Brooks, John "Modern American Society" in John A. Garraty *Historical Viewpoints Notable Articles from American Heritage,* Vol. 2, since 1865. 4th ed., p. 363.

2. BG News, Special Inaugural Supplement, Vol 49 #1 Fri. Sept. 27, 1964, p.1.

3. Jerome Speeches, CAC - President's Office, WTJ III, Box 29, Folder 17. "The Task Ahead" September 12, 1963. p. 2.

4. *The State University - Creator or Conformist.* Bowling Green University Press, WTJ III Inaugural address September 16, 1964. pp. 55 and 60.

5. CAC - President's Office, WTJ III, Box 29, Folder 14. "On Directions, Dreams, and Madness." September 15, 1966. p.8.

6. Ibid. Box 29, Folder 17. "Three Goals for 1969," September 19, 1968. p. 6.

7. BGN, Vol. 50, #23, Oct. 28, 1965, p.1 and Vol. 51, #117, July 27, 1967. p. 1; CAC - President's Office, WTJ III, Box 11, Folder 16.

8. CAC - Interim Report. Bowling Green State University Long-Range Campus Plan. Caudill, Rowlett, and Scott. Oct. 26, 1965. p. 1.

9. Minutes of Board of Trustee (BOT Min.), May 6, 1966.

10. BGN Vol. 51, #22, 23, & 26. Oct. 26 & 27 and Nov. 2, 1966, Passim.

11. Ibid. Vol. 50, #69. Feb. 22, 1966. p. 1 & BOT Min. May 12, 1967.

12. BOT Min. March 3 and September 7, 1967.

13. Ibid. Dec. 14, 1967.

14. Ibid. Jan. 10, May 8, and Oct. 2, 1964 and BGN Vol. 48, #26. Jan. 17, 1964. p. 1.

15. Charles D. Leone and Lloyd J. Buckwell, *Proposals for the Development of Computer Facilities,* BGSU, May, 1969. [BOT Min. Box 19]; BG News. Vol. 47, #30, Feb. 12, 1963, p. 1. & Vol. 48, #50, May 8, 1964, Passim; Bulletin, BGSU, 1967-68, p. 7.

16. BOT Min. Jan. 6, 1967 and May 2, 1969.

17. Ibid. Nov. 19, 1965, March 4, 1966, June 4, 1966, Oct. 7, 1966, Jan. 6, 1967, Aug. 1, 1969 and BGN, Vol. 50, #76, March 4, 1966. p. 2.

18. BOT Min. Jan. 10, 1966 and BGN. Vol. 47, #50, May7, 1963. p. 1 & Vol. 48, #22, Dec. 12, 1963. p. 1.

19. BGN. V. 50, #18. Oct. 20, 1965. p. 1.

20. Donald C. Delong to E.J. Kreischer. CAC Collection, Pres. Office, WTJ, Box9, Folder 17.

21. BGN. Vol. 48, #43, April 14, 1964. p. 4: Vol. 51, #45, Dec. 13, 1966. p. 1.

22. CAC Collection. President's Office, Moore, Box 38, Folder 26.

23. Ibid. Box 47. Manila Envelope.

24. BOT Min.. Nov. 19, 1965, Jan. 7, 1966, March 3, 1967, Sept. 7, 1967, Jan. 24, 1969, May 2, 1969, Aug. 1, 1969, Oct. 10, 1969; BGN, Vol. 53, #98, May 7, 1969, p. 1 & Vol. 54, #44, Jan. 13, 1970. p. 1.

25. BOT Min. March 7, 1969; BGN. Vol. 54, #16, Oct. 21, 1969, p. 1 & Vol. 54, #31, Nov. 13, 1969. pp. 1 & 9.

26. Jerome Speeches, CAC - President's Office, WTJ III, Box 29, Folder 17. "The Task Ahead" September 12, 1963. p. 4.

Notes

Chapter II (cont'd.)

27. Overman, *History,* pp. 193-196; CAC. Governance Documents. *Faculty Charter of Bowling Green State University.* December 1972. pp. 4-10; B.D. Owens and Ray B. Browne, *Teach-in: Viability of Change* (Bowling Green: Bowling Green University Popular Press, 1970), p. 40.

28. CAC Collection. President's Office, WTJ. Box 41, Folder 8.

29. BGN. Vol. 48, #29, February 14, 1965; CAC Collection. Pres. Off., WTJ. Box 29, Folder 13; BOT Min. May 12, 1967.

30. BOT Min. September 27, 1968.

31. CAC Collection. Pres. Off., WTJ. Box 29, Folder 16. Speech To Freshmen, "The Art of Learning". p. 7.

32. CAC, Pres. Off., WTJ. Box 29, Folders 15, 17, & 18; BGN. Vol. 49, #26. Jan. 22, 1965, Passim, Vol. 53, #2. Sept. 26, 1968. p. 3; Sol. M. Linowitz, et al. *Campus Tensions: Analysis and Recommendations. Report of the Special Committee on Compus Tensions.* (Washington, D.C.: American Council on Education, 1970.)

33. BOT Min. March 3, 1967; CAC. Faculty Senate Collection. Box 15, Folder 10.

34. BGN. Vol. 54, #1, Sept. 20, 1969, p. 1, Vol. 54, #15, Oct. 17, 1969, p. 1; BOT Min. Oct. 10, 1969 and Jan. 10, 1970.

35. CAC. Fac Sen Coll. Box 15, Folder 10.

36. MS 376. #13; BGN. Vol. 49, #46. April 27, 1965. pp. 1 & 2.

37. Ibid. #19.

38. BGN. Vol. 51, #13, Oct. 11, 1966, p. 1, #14, Oct. 12, 1966, pp. 1-3, #18, Oct. 19, 1966, p. 1, #19, Oct. 20, 1966, p. 2. #23, Oct. 27, 1966, pp. 1-3, #34, Nov. 16, 1966, p. 1, #44, Dec. 9, 1966, p.1, & #48, Jan. 7, 1967, p. 1; BOT Min. Dec, 14, 1966.

39. BGN. Vol. 49, #7, Oct. 16, 1964, p. 4, #28, Feb. 12, 1965, p. 1, #32, Feb. 20, 1965, p. 4, Vol. 51, #1, June 16, 1966, p. 1, Vol. 52, #78, March 12, 1968, p. 8, Vol. 53, #111, May 29, 1969, p. 1; BOT Min. Sept. 27, 1968, Aug. 1, 1969.

40. WTJ Speeches. Box 29, Folders #14, 1965, 1966, & 1967, #16, 1969, & #17, 1963; BGN. Vol. 48, #1, Sept. 20, 1963, p. 1.

41. BOT Min. March 4, 1966 & Sept. 7, 1967; BGN. Vol. 50, #80, March 16, 1966, p. 1 & March 17, 1966 pp. 1 & 6.

42. BOT Min. Sept. 19, 1968; BGN. Vol. 52, #16, Oct. 13, 1967, p. 21, Vol. 54, #23, Oct. 31, 1969, p. 1 & #25, Nov. 14, 1969, p. 2.

43. BOT Min. Oct. 10, 1969.

44. BGN. Vol. 54, #82, April 7, 1970, p. 2 & Vol. 55, #11, Sept. 17, 1970, p. 5.

45. BOT Min. March 3, 1967.

46. Ibid. July 20, 1965, May 6, 1966, Sept. 7, 1967, & Jan. 24, 1969; BGN. Vol. 50, #12, p. 1.

47. *Bulletin,* 1966-67, p. 6; BGN. Vol. 47, #30, Feb. 12, 1963, p. 1, Vol. 48, #24, Jan. 10, 1964, p. 1, Vol. 49 #14, Nov. 10, 1964, p. 1, Vol. 50, #112, May 18, 1966, p. 1 & Vol. 53, #50, Jan. 24, 1969, p. 6.

Notes

Chapter II (cont'd.)

48. BGN. Vol. 49, #13, Nov. 6, 1964, pp. 1 & 4, #47, April 30, 1965, p. 2, #48, May 4, 1965, p. 2, #49, May 7, 1965, pp. 1 & 2, Vol. 50, #16, Oct. 15, 1965, p. 3, #20, Oct. 22, 1965, p. 2, #82, March 16, 1966, p. 1, #96, April 20, 1966, p. 1, #97, April 21, 1966, Vol. 51, #14, Oct. 12, 1966, p. 1, & Vol. 53, #13, Oct. 16, 1968, p. 1.

49. Ibid. Vol. 49, #27, Jan. 22, 1965. p. 1.

50. Ibid. Vol. 48, #50, May 8, 1964, p. 1, Vol. 51, #34, Nov. 16, 1966, p. 1, #58, Feb. 7, 1967, p. 1, Vol. 50, #78, March 9, 1966, p. 1, #106, May 6, 1966, p. 1, Vol. 51, #84, April 4, 1967, p. 4.

51. Ibid. Vol. 53, #109, May 27, 1969, p. 2. Vol. 54, #31, Nov. 13, 1969, p. 3.

52. Ibid. Vol. 54, #116, June 4, 1970, p. 1 & Vol. 51, #47, Dec. 15, 1966, p. 3.

53. Ibid. Vol. 49, #37, March 16, 1965, p. 1, Vol. 50, #12, Oct. 28, 1965, p. 2, #26, Nov. 3, 1965, pp. 1-2, & #68, Feb. 18, 1966, p. 2.

54. Ibid. Vol. 54, #21, Oct. 29, 1969, p. 1, #35, Nov. 20, 1969, p. 1, #64, Feb. 17, 1970, pp. 1 & 2, #65, Feb. 18, 1970, p. 2, & #66, Feb. 20, 1970, p. 1.

55. MS-376. Items 10 & 10a; Overman, *History,* pp. 154-55; MS-376. Item 7.

56. MS-376. Item 10d; BGN. Vol. 48, #53, May 19, 1964, p. 4, Vol. 51, #5, July, 14, 1966, p. 2, Vol. 52, #1, Sept. 16, 1967, p. 3.

57. MS-376, Item 10e & 10f. BGN. Vol. 49, #16, Nov. 17, 1964, p. 1, Vol. 50, #72, Feb. 25, 1966, p. 5, Vol. 51, #15, Oct. 14, 1966, p. 2.

58. Jerome Speeches. Sept. 12, 1963, p. 1.

59. MS-376. #10b.

60. BOT Min. Jan. 10, 1964; Faculty Research Committee Files, May 8 & 21, 1964 and Nov. 20, 1964; Jerome Speeches, Sept. 14, 1967; FRC, Oct. 29, 1964; BOT Min., May 1, 1970, Oct. 29, 1964, Feb. 9, 1968, & July 7, 1971.

61. MS-376. #6, 9a & c; BOT Min. March 3, 1967, Dec. 14, 1967, May 10, 1968, May 2, 1969, Oct. 10, 1969, & May 1, 1970.

62. BOT Min. May 10, 1968 & Oct. 10, 1969; MS-376. #3, 3a. & 4; BGN, Vol. 53, #45, Jan. 16, 1969, p. 1, #46, Jan. 17, 1969, p. 1, #47, Jan. 21, 1969, p. 1, #49, Jan. 23, 1969, p. 1, #50, Jan. 24, 1969, p. 1, #52, Jan. 29, 1969, p. 1, #56, Feb. 6, 1969, p. 1., #71, March 4, 1969, p. 1, & #90, April 21, 1969, p. 7.

63. MS-376, #6a; BOT Min. Jan. 10, 1964, May 8, 1964, Oct. 2, 1964, Oct. 7, 1966, Nov. 8, 1966, Jan. 6, 1967, March 6, 1970, May 1, 1970, & July 10, 1970.

CHAPTER III

"...TO THE CAMPUS SCENE"
The Relevance or Irrelevance of Times Past

Building in the 1960s — Jerome Library

CHAPTER III

"...TO THE CAMPUS SCENE"
The Relevance or Irrelevance of Times Past

As pointed out at the beginning of Chapter II, William T. Jerome not only assumed the mantle of president of Bowling Green but almost simultaneously the tensions of a changing and restless society. What was the temper of the times, and what were the root causes? Much soul searching occurred during the period over what was happening, and a great deal of research has transpired since. From all of this some general conclusions can be drawn.

The United States, Seymour Martin Lipset argues in his book *The First New Nation,* has been both guided and pulled by the twin dynamics of individualism/achievement and egalitarianism. The period of the latter 1960s was one in which egalitarianism was the ascendant force in the nation as seen in the civil rights movement, consumer and environmental concerns, the beginnings of the women's movement, and the anti-Vietnam War activities.[1] These forces permeated the whole society including the youth of college age. Coupled with these influences were a number that were more directly of concern to the university population. A report released in 1970 by the American Council on Education theorized that the causes of disruption were: a generational conflict; a feeling by teenagers that society viewed them as immature and thus socially 'irrelevant'; a conviction that educational practices and curriculum were obsolete and thus not relevant; a general decline in the acceptance of authority as being justified; and, the emergence of a social malaise theory in which universities were viewed as either fair game for destruction or as a place to initiate a cure.[2] In sum, students "...are discontented not only with colleges and universities, but also with American society, and they see a connection of basic failings between the two."³ The study pointed out that the majority of students were relatively content, but cautioned that "Whatever the size of the discontented minority, its members are...among the brightest, most experienced, widely read, and articulate young Americans,"⁴ The *BG News* in 1966 reported on a study which cited some additional factors in shaping the current college generation. The five key ones were: the record number of students going to college; their use of psychology as an everyday tool; their search for new "working with people" careers; the impact of affluence; and the disruptive pressures of the draft.⁵ While still other factors have been hypothesized for the tensions and turmoil of the period the foregoing encompass many of the elements that influenced events on the Bowling Green campus.

Tensions? Turmoil? Disturbances?

While the overall impression that emanated from the Jerome years was one of challenge and change at many levels most of the period was filled by the normal daily, mundane events that characterize a university campus. These commonplace aspects of college life, while not the momentous events that come immediately to mind, often become collectively the aura that lingers on over the years. Among them were athletic, recreational, and social activities.

The beginning of Jerome's presidency was bracketed by two retirements that brought an end to a major athletic age at Bowling Green. Just prior to his arrival Harold Anderson had stepped down after over twenty years as basketball coach, although he continued as Athletic Director. Two years later Doyt Perry retired after a decade as "the winningest" football coach in America, and assumed the Athletic directorship from Anderson. No one during the rest of the 1960s was able to gain the national reputation that those two had held. In spite of the loss of the two, Bowling Green continued generally to do well in all of its intercollegiate sports. Although it garnered only six league championships during the period, twelve individuals in five different sports received All-American recognition. These twelve included: Howard Komives (Basketball) who in 1963-64 led the nation in scoring; Sid Sink who won the NCAA Steeplechase in 1970 and was the only person other than Jesse Owens to win six Central Collegiate Conference titles; and Michael Weger who in 1965 was the first Bowling Green football player to win major college All-American honors. When President Jerome arrived on campus there were nine men's and three women's intercollegiate sports. In the Fall of 1964 a club team composed of five Canadians and fourteen Americans played the university's first hockey game. The team, organized in anticipation of the completion of the ice arena, became an intercollegiate competitor in 1969. Two years earlier two other sports, soccer and lacrosse, were raised to the intercollegiate level as well.[6]

While the Jerome administration was not a memorable period overall athletically, it was one of major importance in the development of athletic facilities. The bulk of the athletic complex east of Yount Road was planned and constructed during the late 1960s. This development included the Ice Arena, Steller Field, Perry Stadium, Whittaker Track, Creason Golf Course (first nine holes), Keefe Tennis Courts, Cochrane Soccer Field, the Cross Country course, and the Intramural Playing fields. The last named facility helped assist in the expansion of the Intramural Program. In 1963 some 3000 Greek and independent students participated in twenty different sports while by 1970 some 6000 took part in twenty-nine team and individual activities. The program was flexible so that different sports were available as participant demand dictated, running from table tennis and curling to the perennial football and baseball.[7]

As the investment in intercollegiate athletics grew faculty concern over its role surfaced. A four-member committee was created which reported in August of 1968. The report asserted that the faculty role in athletic policy was minimal and that there was a need for serious discussion on the basic philosophy of the university toward intercollegiate athletics.[8]

Campus groups and activities multiplied as rapidly as the enrollment. Departmental and interest clubs plus honoraries served the interests of many students. During the 1960s local honoraries were replaced by national equivalent ones with the most significant being the conversion of the fifty-year-old Book and Motor Society to the national honorary society of Phi

Kappa Phi. Interest groups increased from approximately forty in 1963 to around sixty in 1970. They reflected the conventional - choral groups, departmental - Chemical Journal Club, and the times - Americans for Democratic Action and Student Religious Liberals. Fraternities and sororities in their third decade on campus were buffeted seriously, as will be noted later, but continued active. In the Spring of 1964 two new Greek events were introduced which added to the traditional functions. They were the Phi Kappa Tau "Bed Race" and the Beta Theta Pi "Beta Little 500."[9]

Entertainment and recreation is as much a part of a university tradition almost as the alma mater, ivy clad walls, and eccentric professors. A perennial problem was that of whether students should be offered as "cultural" events those programs/artists deemed best or those that they wanted. *The BG News* in its pages and the students with their feet supported the latter position. While Bowling Green had no Mory's each college generation has had its favorite spots. During the 1960's there were four locally that were especially patronized. One was a haunt of long standing, Howard's, which had opened its doors in 1933. The other three were all products of the 1960s, The Northgate Inn, the Canterbury Inn (CIs), and J. Alfred's all of which were gone by the late 1970s, and replaced by other popular spots. In February 1969 a quite different addition was made to the entertainment and recreation scene when a mimeographed twelve page sheet giving a daily schedule of events was published. In time this emerged as a publication known as *The Green Sheet*.[10]

Challenges and Changes

"...Just because values change...doesn't mean there are no basic rules students have to adhere to."[11]

A song popular at the time said that "times are a changing," and such was the case. Each year of the Jerome administration seemed to bring more demands for change not just from the university administration, but within the entire university community. Some of the alterations were of an evolutionary nature while others seemed, at least at the time, to be almost revolutionary.

Housing and the rules related to residential living gradually were modified from 1963 into the early 1970s. Until 1967 the university required that all undergraduate women and all freshman and sophomore men were required to live on campus. In that year several modifications were made including changing the word require to expect and giving upper class women the right to live off-campus with parental permission. During the Jerome years hours for women also witnessed a mutation. In 1963 residence hours Monday through Thursday were 10 p.m. for freshmen and 11 p.m. for upperclassmen; Friday and Saturday 1 a.m. for all classes; and, Sunday 11 p.m. for all classes. Additionally, there were hours when women had to be in their rooms which was roughly an hour after dorm hours. In 1966 hours for freshmen and upperclass women were lengthed by two hours on week days and an hour on weekends, and then in 1968 hours for women were dropped although hours for closing of dormitories were kept. These changes in hours occurred with a minimum of student harassment. An ironic outgrowth of the granting of no hours occurred in October 1968 when a small group of students held a sit-in at the Falcon's Nest protesting that no university social or food facilities remained open after 11 p.m. although students were allowed to be out. This led in January to an experiment in which the Rathskellar in The Commons remained open all night - an experiment that failed owing to lack of patronage.[12]

Another housing regulation, "calling hours/open house," was modified, but only after confrontation. The *AWS Handbook* of 1963 said that "Men callers may be entertained in lounges" from 1 to 5 p.m. daily and 7 to 10 p.m. Monday through Thursday and 7 p.m. to 1 a.m. Friday and Saturday. In March 1969 the issue of open houses which had arisen in 1968 erupted. An open house as described in the 1970 *AWS Handbook* was "...a scheduled period of time during which the entire (living) unit (not including showers and rest rooms) may be open to invited guests...of both sexes..."[13] Early in March some 250 men and women students held a sit-in in Rodgers Residence Hall to call attention to a student wish for Friday and Saturday night and Sunday afternoon open houses including the right to have individual room doors closed and lights turned off. (Attendant with this demand was one for dormitory "autonomy" which will be discussed later.) The day following the sit-in a Resident Assistant charged with encouraging the protest was relieved of his duties. That and the momentum already generated led to an open forum developing in front of Williams Hall during which the Student Council President, Nick Licate, and others demanded open houses. Coincidental with the forum was an imminent meeting of the Board of Trustees. The decision was made to attend in mass the board meeting and when it convened later in the day an estimated 800 students were present. Following the meeting the Chair of the Board, Donald Simmons, opened the meeting to questions whereupon, after a short time, Licate took over control of the microphone. President Jerome and the Board responded by walking out of the meeting. The next issue of the *BG News* proclaimed "Licate acted well" and continued by congratulating him for helping students "...realize that they can control their environment." The immediate outcome was twofold. A number of students involved in the Rodgers' sit-in were placed on probation and the administration agreed to allow a maximum of two open hours per week with the approval of the dorm residents, but with doors open and lights on.[14]

During the 1960s a number of other approaches to residence life evolved. As the number and capacity of dormitories grew along with the enrollment, socially and even educationally the old all campus approach to student programming was altered. Increasingly many more activities were centered in the dorm. Some residence halls even were used for specific purposes such as Harshman D with a bilingual floor, McDonald North for international students, and Prout Hall as an honors' dorm. A major innovation was instituted in 1966 when students were afforded the opportunity to submit preferential requests for the residence hall and the roommate of their choice. As seemed true of most changes during this era there were always some that caused a flap. One such was the decision in 1968 to require that all housing contracts be signed for the academic year. The Student Council debated the matter and voted 44-0 urging students to refuse to sign, and the *BG News* ran a front page headline "BOYCOTT!" Discussions followed and the policy was modified to require only freshmen and sophomores to sign such contracts. This controversy reflected the adversarial attitude that had arisen as well as the seemingly increased desire of students to move off campus.[15]

A move off campus was contemplated and actively pursued by members of the Greek system during the last four years of the Jerome administration. The momentum originated, at least in part, from discrimination in housing questions raised by the Ohio Civil Rights Commission in 1966. Starting in the Spring of 1967 the university began working with various Greek groups on the concept of creating a corporation that could own and develop a Greek Village. In December Jerome reported to the Board of Trustees on the progress being made and in February 1968 fourteen fraternities and sororities formed the Greek Village Development Corporation. In May the Trustees officially approved the establishment of a Village with the proviso that all rules applying to the university and its housing be obeyed. The next two years were spent futilely in searching for and procuring a suitable location. In July 1970 the Board was told that the project was in "a state of limbo." However, movement of a different sort had occurred just two months earlier when the Trustees had approved on a one year trial basis the move of Beta Theta Pi Fraternity off campus and into an apartment building.[16]

Many other rules and regulations were moderated or tempered in nature or application. The *AWS Handbooks* for 1963 and 1970 indicate this. In 1963 there were twelve pages devoted to policies and regulations while by 1970 only half that space was devoted to them. Two excellent examples of this, in addition to hour regulations, were those on smoking and attire. In 1963 three paragraphs were devoted to smoking, but in 1970 only one sentence appeared. The 1963 Handbook on dress had seven regulations listed, one of which stated that "Shorts, Bermudas, jeans, slacks, etc. are not to be worn in classrooms, administrative or faculty offices, the Library, the Union except on the first floor, or in residence hall dining rooms except at the specified times." In 1970 two sentences covered the subject. The catalog statement on marriage by a student further reflects the changing times. In 1963 a statement said in part "A student who marries while enrolled...is required to inform the Dean of Men or the Dean of Women immediately. Failure to comply...will be considered an automatic withdrawal...and the student will be dropped...immediately without refund of fees." In 1967 the statement to inform remained but concluded "...only in this

way will the university know of address changes.'' Finally, in
1971 the statement was ''A student who marries while enrolled...
is requested to inform the Dean of Students immediately.''[17]

While the question of beer and drugs on campus was not
unique to the 1960s its growing acceptance was. Students arriv-
ing in the Fall of 1963 found that the university had shifted its
policy on alcohol consumed off campus to conform with state
law, and thereby placed responsibility on the individual for
sobriety rather than the group where it had long been lodged. In
early 1966 a policy was approved that allowed Greek and
residential groups to buy 3.2 beer for off campus functions. As
might be expected, in 1967 the Student Council passed a resolution recommending the serving of 3.2 beer on campus. President Jerome responded that he wanted a broader indication of
support than just Student Council. In May 1967 a campus
referendum was held asking whether or not students favored
selling beer on campus, and if so where. The results were 1570
for and 1355 against with only the Rathskeller being approved
as a location and the Union being turned down by a two to one
vote. In the Fall of 1967 a similar survey was taken with the
same outcome - the vote being 4244 for and 3045 against. Further action was slow in coming, but in January 1969 the Board
of Trustees with modest support from President Jerome voted
five to three to start selling 3.2 beer in the Fall in a designated
area of The Union. University policy on drugs did not alter over
the years, but the attitude of the *BG News* did. In early 1964 a
student was arrested for possession of marijuana and the *News*
in an editorial cautioned its readers about the use of hallucino-
genic drugs. In March of 1970 following some arrests for the
same offense the *News* editorially asked ''is this justice?'' and
argued that marijuana was not a narcotic and those possessing it
should not be treated as if it were a drug.[18]

Us and Them

''...You for some reason, do not wish to recognize that you are
junior partners in this education undertaking.''

''It is not a question of asking anyone to give us rights. It is a
case of exerting those rights we already have.''[19]

As the decade of the 1960s wore on students increasingly
asserted that they had a right to take part in or, even in some

cases, to control their own education. This conviction led to disagreement and conflict among students and between students and faculty and administrators.

During the first four years of the Jerome administration the bulk of the discontent was among the students themselves. A poll of 1900 students early in 1964 showed that eighty percent of them felt that the university administration was receptive to their views, but only thirty-one percent of them believed that the Student Council really represented their ideas. The question of representativeness of student government organizations pervaded student opinion through the whole period. Criticism of the Student Council and the Association of Women Students (AWS) began in 1965 and accelerated so that by 1969-70 the *BG News* wrote them off as "irrelevant." Another indication of this attitude was seen in the decline of voters in student government elections from 47.4% in 1965 to 8.0% in 1969.

From 1964 until 1969 Student Council was variously attacked as unrepresentative and undemocratic. The method of choosing members of the Council was changed twice with neither modification seeming to satisfy entirely. At one point in 1969 a short crisis arose when the body agreed to seat two representatives of the Black Student Union. The Interfraternity Council challenged the constitutionality of the action and appealed to the Student Court. Before the court acted the vote was reversed, but the court did call for a new representation plan. Emanating from this came the suggestion that Student Council be abolished and a Student Assembly be created —an idea that had some support. However, the modification made was to keep the Council but make its members all ones elected at large. One other intra-student dispute concerned the academic requirements for student and class officers. The rule in 1963 was that a student to be eligible to hold such offices had to have a 2.5 grade point average (GPA) or better. By early 1966 this was being challenged as elitist and over the duration of the next year was reduced first to 2.25 and then only to "good standing."[20]

Similarly, AWS came under attack. In late 1964 and early 1965 a number of women students questioned the need for mandatory membership and the need for its rules. This criticism led to a revision of its constitution by the end of the academic year. In November 1968 charges that due process in judicial proceedings was not being assured brought a call from Student Council for an investigation. While the latter did not happen, AWS supported by the Dean of Women did denounce the Council for infringing on its autonomy. The continuing woes of AWS were further evident when in 1969 the *BG News* editorially stated that it was not endorsing any candidate for the AWS presidency "...because of the basic irrelevancy of the organization."[21]

The 1964 student poll that indicated trust in the administration's openness to change was reciprocal. Between 1964 and 1966 the university altered substantially the role of students in the handling of discipline cases. Initially, except for the enforcement of residence hall rule infractions, students dealt only with campus traffic/parking matters. All other types of cases were handled by the personnel deans. By the late 1960s several alternatives had been developed which in most cases gave students the choice of being tried by a personnel dean or panel or by their peers. A major difference of philosophy clouded one phase of this cooperative handling of discipline cases. The personnel deans averred that in some instances counseling was much more salutary than litigation, and, therefore, ought to be used. At the time of the Rodgers autonomy controversy several students accused the administration when counseling was done of denying students their right of due process. The university did not yield on this point, however.[22]

The furor and turmoil existing on many campuses led a number of national university oriented organizations to issue in the Summer of 1967 a "Joint Statement on Rights and Freedoms of Students." It prompted the following resolution in December from the Board of Trustees:

> "WHEREAS, the climate on university campuses these days is one marked by increasing agitation and demands for change on the part of students; and
>
> WHEREAS, it is important that we create a milieu for change in the relationships between students, faculty and administration at this University that will take place in a planned and orderly manner;

THEREFORE BE IT RESOLVED, that we must keep in mind, as we plan for change, the educational goals of this institution and the changing conditions of today's students and today's world."[23]

The resolution expressed clearly the views of the President and the newly appointed Vice President for Student Affairs, James G. Bond. Rather quickly, however, strains began to appear as differences over the implementation of cooperation and change arose. President Jerome emphasized that student participation was a privilege and not a right while student leaders retorted that it was both. Increasingly the administration was challenged on these grounds. In the Spring of 1967 Student Council disputed the right of the university to review and even veto the decisions of the Organizations Board concerning the recognition of new student groups. In the Fall Council censured the administration for preventing the rather newly formed Students for a Democratic Society (SDS) from circulating a beer survey on campus, and that same Council also abolished the long standing position of faculty advisor. In October 1968 Student Council adopted a "Student Bill of Rights" which baldly asserted such rights as those of due process, of determining the rules under which one lives, of participating in peaceful demonstrations, and of being subject only to rules that have been fully and clearly formulated, published, and distributed. The ultimate challenge to the administration was the enactment of Student Council Bills Two and Twenty which granted autonomy to the residence halls. These bills helped encourage the open house policy sit-in at Rodgers in March 1969, and became the basis for student support for those involved. The Student Council president, Nick Licate, assured the students that they had acted legally and that, therefore, Student Council would not permit any of them to be expelled by the university. As noted earlier, confrontation occurred with the President and the Board in an open meeting and some accommodation was made on the open house issue. However, the university did not accept the right of Student Council to grant autonomy. The firm administrative position led to an acceleration of the feeling that Student Council was powerless.

A month after the Rodgers sit-in in March 1969 another incident flared up that further strained student-administrative relations. The university suspended nine students who had been charged with narcotics offenses by a grand jury. In time only two of the nine remained as fulltime students and therefore involved in the suspension process. A number of students and faculty appealed for reinstatement of the two pending the outcome of the trial. Others argued that the students were being subjected to double jeopardy. The two individuals successfully appealed their suspension but President Jerome over-ruled the decision stating his conviction that their continued presence was not in the best interests of the university.[24] The events of March and April engendered a *BG News* editorial that "Student Government is a hoax...an intricate, complex and highly efficient system of diverting students from getting anything of true value accomplished."[25] A year later the opinion still prevailed in a position paper signed by the Student Council President, Vice President and others. In it they stated the Council was "...irrelevant to the university governance process and harmful to the educational process."[26] These conclusions pushed student leaders and even President Jerome to recommend by 1970 the creation of a university or community council composed of students, faculty, and administrators.[27]

While this conviction grew that traditional student government was futile, the belief that students had a right to a voice continued. This certainty was reflected in various approaches pursued over the years. A major difficulty, as pointed out by President Jerome, was the imbalance of power between the faculty and its Senate and the student body and its Council. It seemed axiomatic to many students that if 600 plus faculty had rights delegated to them that 13,000 students should have the same, or, at the very least, they should have access to the decision makers. Well before many students gave up on student government the access route was being pursued in a number of ways with considerable eventual success.

Between the Winter of 1965 and the Spring of 1970 the Faculty Senate was constantly importuned to open itself to student opinion. The first battle was simply to permit the *BG News* to attend and report on meetings of the Senate; a privilege granted in early 1966. Student Council next requested permission for its president or a representative to attend meetings which was acceded to in December 1966. By the 1969-70 academic year the Student Council President was submitting bills passed by his organization to Faculty Senate for collaborative action. When the Senate turned down a student bill charges of hypocrisy were leveled at the faculty. A final step was taken in April 1970 when the Faculty Senate voted to seat four undergraduate and two graduate students with full voting rights. A second line pursued was to obtain a voice in administrative and faculty personnel decisions. While some debate occurred earlier the issue came to a head in February 1970 when the *BG News* broke a story that four instructors, who were reputedly good teachers, had been denied tenure. The furor was sharp but brief as efforts were made to force reconsideration of the decisions through a futilely attempted registration boycott of History Department classes - a department in which two of the four faculty taught. Two more successful efforts involved the use of teaching evaluation forms as a segment of the tenure and promotion process and the introduction of students onto departmental executive/evaluation committees. In late Winter 1970 the College of Business determined that it would use college wide teaching evaluation forms - a pattern later followed by others. Student participation in departmental policy making had begun in some areas as early as the 1967-68 school year. It was given added emphasis in April 1970 when the Faculty Senate endorsed the principle of student involvement, but a number of departments continued to reject the idea.[28]

A whole new area of student participation in university governance was opened in January 1968 when Governor James Rhodes suggested that one student be added as a non-voting member to each Board of Trustees. The idea met considerable resistance and was not enacted into law. However, the concept appealed to student leaders, and the Student Council began a campaign for a non-voting seat on the Board. In January 1970 the Board refused on legal grounds to accept a student, but did extend an invitation for a student representative to attend all meetings and express student views.[29]

At the municipal and state level student involvement was mixed. In an effort to improve relations the Bowling Green

Exchange Club in the Fall of 1968 created a discussion group composed of townspeople, students, and faculty to exchange ideas and opinions. At the end of the second year the program was ended by its sponsor owing to a lack of student interest, involvement, and attendance. At the state level Bowling Green student government engaged itself briefly on two different occasions. In the Spring of 1967 the financial support for higher education was faltering sufficiently that a number of university student governments decided to found a lobbying organization called the Ohio Confederation of State University Governments. Thomas Liber who was student body president became the first, and last, chair of the group. Two years later state student governments reacted negatively to two proposals of Governor Rhodes that called for increasing student fees and creating regional university administrative areas. The current student body president and other members of student government lobbied in Columbus on these issues.[30]

Justice and Social Concern

A college or university "...must strive as never before to become a bastion of high purpose, a goad to the public conscience, an implacable enemy of the false, the inhumane, and the unjust."[31]

As noted at the beginning of Chapter Two the years from late 1963 on were ones of accelerated political and social awareness and action. At Bowling Green that deepening of conscience developed sporadically and not with unanimity. The concerns mirrored those found nationally such as; women's rights, discrimination, the environment, minorities, and war. As time passed some of the concerned became more active and even extreme which in turn produced countervailing forces. For much of the period the various issues kept their separate identity but as 1970 began a number of them tended to merge together into a common demand for change.

At the end of his first year in office Jerome was faced with his first major social issue. In May 1964 the Ohio Civil Rights Commission initiated a study of alleged discriminatory practices by fraternities and sororities using university housing. In the Fall the commission asked the university to institute a policy in which housing contracts included a provision forbidding discrimination and providing that if such were found that the contract would be void. Additionally, the university was asked to issue a statement that all vacancies in any facility would be filled without regard to race, color, or religion. While the president complained about bureaucracy such policies and contracts were in use for the 1965-66 academic year, and had the endorsement of the Interfraternity Council. By 1966 the official policy was clearly one of non-discrimination, but the question of Greek discrimination and then that of minority treatment in general continued.[32]

As the national awareness of blacks intensified so did that of those on campus. In early Spring 1968 black leaders called for an active recruitment of black students. Vice President Bond supported this call and cited the fact that there were no blacks on the faculty and that there were only approximately one hundred black students. The 1968-69 school year witnessed the active appearance of a new organization — the Black Student Union (BSU) which in February made its first "demands." It sought and was initially granted two seats on the Student Council, but once the constitutionality of the action was challenged the vote was rescinded amid some rancorous racial slurs. Later in the Spring the BSU requested the administration to increase both the number of black faculty and students and to develop a facility on campus in which blacks could have a feeling of belonging. During the Summer of 1969 the university actively recruited black students and also formed the Student Development Program as a means of aiding those who needed help in the transition from high school to college. Shortly after classes resumed in the Fall it was announced that The Rathskeller, a student hangout in The Commons, was to be converted into "a soul-jazz environment for black students." While generally supported this move too elicited some negative response. In April 1970 student unrest on a number of Ohio campuses erupted. Among the most active were blacks who sought wide-sweeping changes. At Bowling Green following similar actions at Ohio State the BSU made on April 30 eight "demands" of the university. They included calls for: an increase of blacks to ten percent of the student body along with support services for them; the employment of more black faculty and administrators; initiation of a Black Studies curriculum; recognition of BSU and financial support for it; creation of a committee to evaluate and reform the treatment of black athletes and off-campus renters; the disarming of campus police; and, a promise of no reprisals for those supportive of the demands. The document concluded by demanding an immediate start of negotiations, or a program would be initiated to stop any further enrollment of blacks in what was labeled a "white racist institution." Discussion on the proposals was just underway when the shootings at Kent State heightened immeasureably tensions on the campus.

The second major issue that pervaded much of the late 1960s and early 1970s was the involvement of the United States in Southeast Asia. A consciousness of the military escalation in Vietnam and its potential implications emerged slowly on campus. From the Fall of 1964 until the late Spring of 1966 the general tenor of the campus including that of the *BG News* was one of support for the efforts of the government. In April and May of 1966 the first major discussion of the war occurred. In April the Student Council endorsed the circulation of a petition which called on the United States to take the initiative in resolving the differences between North and South Vietnam, and in May a Vietnam Week was held in which both sides of the controversy were presented. The 1966-67 academic year saw a gradual increase in the debate, but was relatively free of major controversy. From the Fall of 1967 onward the tempo of objections to the war markedly increased. A "Day of Dissent" held in October attracted some 500 to 700 people. During the Winter and Spring of 1968 such anti-war speakers as Dick Gregory, Max Lerner, and Tom Hayden appeared, and the year was capped in May with an anti-war protest held during the Annual ROTC Review. 1968-69 followed a pattern similar to the previous year; speakers—Julian Bond, George McGovern, and Jerry Rubin; and, special events—a silent protest vigil, a Draft Week, and a controlled protest at the ROTC Review. October 15, 1969 was declared nationally as the day for a Vietnam Moratorium. Student Council voted to support the day and to cancel classes. When the Faculty Senate opposed cancellation, the Council and the *BG News* called for a boycott of classes.

Meetings held during the 15th were addressed by President Jerome and by a number of faculty and students, and were generally well attended. On April 15, 1970 another national rally day was held, but the event on campus was only sparsely attended. One other war related issue surfaced in January 1970; namely, the academic value and place of ROTC in the university. The Student Council launched a study of the question which resulted in an ROTC Bill that recommended the discontinuance of credit for ROTC courses. The bill was referred to the Curriculum Committee of the College of Business for the appropriate academic review. When the appointed member of the Student Council was asked to testify in May he informed the committee that the Council did not want to participate any longer in "...meaningless forms of Committee governance." A few days later the Council officially dropped the whole probe.[34]

A couple of other causes engrossed the campus for shorter periods of time during the Jerome years. The president was greatly interested in environmental matters and thus generated a continuing if often low level interest in the subject. The culmination of such concern was the university wide Environmental Teach-in that was held during April 1970. While much of the leadership was local, the program was kicked off by Ralph Nader. The 1969-70 school year witnessed the beginning of an issue that ran well into the 1970s; namely, the demand for birth control pills to be dispensed, upon request, by the physicians at the Student Health Center. AWS and the *BG News* both campaigned for the idea, but as of the Spring of 1970 the official policy remained that the Center would neither stock nor dispense "the pill", but would write prescriptions for out of state married students.[35]

The Foreshadowing of May 1970

"We should not be talking about university reform, but instead, openly talking about university revolution."

"...I hope that at the very least we would not be so foolish as to impose the type of restraints on the young which would lessen their options and ours in fashioning tomorrow's world. But constraints there must be..."[36]

The disturbances and disruptions on university campuses that began at Berkeley caused faculty and administrators—especially President Jerome — growing concern. The major anxiety was how by consensus or code to delineate fairly the line between academic freedom and license. The earliest effort at clarification came with the adoption in July 1965 by the Board of Trustees of a Faculty Senate resolution guaranteeing the right of free speech as long as it did not infringe on the rights of others or disrupt classroom activity. A lull then followed as fewer campus demonstrations lessened the seeming urgency to develop a broad policy.

A new spur to action arose in the Fall of 1966 with the founding of an SDS chapter on campus. While its membership creed seemed moderate - all individuals should be involved in decisions concerning themselves and that nothing is immune from criticism - it had a reputation for radicalism. The first president averred that SDS was tied intellectually to the New Left, but had no political ties on the left. The then Chair of the Political Science Department described the student members as idealists concerned with civil rights and university governance. He added that their manifesto Call To Arms "...is a model of non-communication, more baffling than informative, but it has not the slightest trace of Communism, Russian or Chinese." In spite of these assurances concern persisted.[37]

In May 1967 President Jerome sounded out the alumni, students, and faculty on how best to protect the rights of the majority from the tyranny of the minority. The answer was clear - no consensus existed on either whether there was a problem or, if one, on how to handle it. Even though the university was in seeming disarray over policy approaches to disorders, the state legislature suddenly in the Spring of 1968 filled the void. Senate Bill 468 squarely placed responsibility on the Board of Trustees to regulate the physical plant and the conduct of individuals and to promulgate the necessary regulations to accomplish that end. While the intrusion of outside pressures was disliked, the Board requested the university administration to develop the regulations necessary to meet the legislative mandate. The need for a clearer policy became apparent in late May when a controversy centering on protests at the ROTC Review erupted. Charges of disruption on the one hand and of a lack of protection of the demonstrators on the other rent the campus. The more immediate problem was resolved through an investigation, and the longer policy approach was addressed in a document submitted to the Board in September 1968 entitled "Procedures and Regulations Governing Students, Staff, & Visitors." At the same meeting the Board was informed of the difficulty of dealing with individuals who dispense inflammatory and/or obscenely worded materials on campus, and, hence, of the practical problems of enforcement of any policy which seems to infringe on the rights of a person.

The initial board approved procedures were viewed as only a partial step. The 1968 statement did not include faculty because the Faculty Senate had objected to inclusion holding that the Faculty Charter, the Tenure Statement, and its own 1965 Statement on Freedom of Political Expression were sufficient. During the following year compromises were worked out which gained the approval of the Senate for the ultimate statement adopted by the Board in October 1969 as "Procedures & Regulations Governing Students, Staff, Faculty, & Visitors." While the 1968 document included students it did not deal with the question of implementation of the procedures. The refinement of a broad based student code was a long process, but by the Spring of 1970 an acceptable one had been hammered out.[38]

President Jerome found the process of working with an often contentious faculty and student body merely frustrating, but his confrontations with the *BG News* approached by 1968-69 being ulcerous. During his last years two tacks taken by the paper created strained relations between the News and many others including Jerome. The differences centered around a pugnacious editorial policy and the increased use of language viewed by many as obscene. In June 1969 the President was presented with a petition signed by several hundred faculty and students protesting the editorial bias and journalistic license of the paper, and asking that the withholding of university financial support be studied. The criticism was partially countered by the Student Publications Committee which held that the paper reflected the temper of the times; one which demanded strong criticism of the establishment. The next move occurred with the publication of the October 3, 1969 edition of the *BG News*. The decades old masthead "Serving a Growing University Since 1920" was replaced with "An Independent Student Voice" which the editor stated he hoped had a significance greater than just a cosmetic one. In March 1970 the President in a letter to the editor of the News indicated that financial support for the paper might be cut at some future point since "...for the life of me I can't see how a student newspaper can justify being subsidized by the very persons it chooses to villify." However, the New's independent line or as Jerome once referred to its policy as "...the SDS line in its hostility to 'the administration' and its disregard for factual, objective reporting" persevered. While the controversy of the News carrying "...its editorial page to the treatment of the front page news"[39] raged on, a second issue, that of obscenity, erupted. Initially, the criticism was local and elicited the editorial response that obscenity was not a four letter word, but war, famine, violence, and racism. The issue escalated, however, in February 1970 when after several state legislators objected to "gross obscenities" appearing in the *OU Post* Wood County Representative, Charles Kurfess, charged that the News was also guilty of vulgarity and "gutter tripe," and urged it to use some discretion. The News response was twofold: 1) legislators should not infringe on their freedom, and 2) they did use discretion, but in relation to the youth audience that were their readers. In spite of his reservations about the paper, Jerome wrote Kurfess a letter assuring him that the educational leaders of the state would protect the vital interests of higher education and imploring him to have "...faith in your educational leaders — and particularly in your youth." The obscenity question continued to vex the university community, however.[40]

The Days of May - 1970

A crescendo of protests on university campuses throughout Ohio and the nation marked the days from the middle of April into early May. While disruptions had bubbled up periodically in the state during the past couple years, nothing approximated the contagion that swept from Miami to Ohio University to Ohio State to Kent. Several common concerns — ROTC, black rights, and campus police—were in the forefront of all of the protests. As the agitation worsened Governor Rhodes activated the National Guard which tended to further exacerbate the situation. Potential difficulty at Bowling Green surfaced when the BSU on April 30th submitted its "demands" to the university administration. Conferring on the issues was going on when the news of the shooting of students at Kent State by National Guardsmen reached the campus in early afternoon on Monday, May 4th. The next week was one of many rallies, much debate, and considerable tension. On Tuesday morning the 5th a memorial service was held for those killed at Kent State and those present—students, administrators, and faculty—pledged themselves to avoid violence. A system of student marshalls was developed with which most cooperated. In the afternoon of the 5th the Faculty Senate met with some 2000 present at the Student Forum and voted to cancel classes on the 6th so that various activities honoring the Kent State dead could be held. In addition, the Senate passed resolutions condemning violence and supporting the BSU requests for affirmative recruiting and a black studies program. That meeting in the opinion of President Jerome was "...the turning point in terms of the disturbances of the week putting things into a constructive vein...."[41] On Wednesday the 6th another large rally on the mall in front of Williams Hall discussed plans for a candle light march through downtown Bowling Green for that evening. At 8:30 p.m. the silent march began with an estimated 7000 to 8000 university and townspeople participating in what all agreed was an emotional experience. The major development of the following day was agreement between the administration and BSU on a plan to upgrade black enrollment and total university awareness of black culture. The scheme involved a major financial commitment by the university along with positive administrative action. Early Sunday afternoon, May 10th, the Faculty Senate met in a special session off campus to consider various academic options for the remainder of the school year. After much debate the Senate voted to permit students the option of converting any or all courses to a S-U basis and endorsed the offering of a number of supplemental courses on current concerns under the aegis of what was called the New University (New U). The following day at a noon rally on the mall some 4000 students were given the outline of the New U. and told that the first classes would start three days later. As a result of the shooting of students at Jackson State three more rallies occurred, but the intensity level was markedly lower. During the remainder of the Spring Quarter some 125 New U. courses met with students and faculty intermingling freely in groups of three or four to fifty or more. All told an estimated 3500 individuals participated in some manner.[42]

Bowling Green was the only residential state university not to close for some period during May, 1970. Much pride evolved from that fact and considerable debate as to why it happened. The post mortems were many and diverse, but some consensus did emerge. Foremost among the positive forces at work was President Jerome who many felt made his last hours as President his greatest. He demonstrated leadership, perseverance, flexibility, firmness, and openness both in open forums and private planning sessions. His personal involvement was complemented by the shared managerial system that he had fostered over seven years with fellow administrators and faculty. His style had also helped make the "...campus a more human place to work and study," and thus a place where "...the students turned *to* the administration, turned *to* the faculty, and *to* other students rather than against 'the' university." Another factor was the composition of the student body, the nature of which was partially seen in its responsiveness to responsible leadership and in its sincerity and concern as reflected in many of the letters received by the President.[43]

While the university community and many of its friends were gratified with the outcome of events, there were others who were far from pleased. Even though many of the letters that the president's office received were favorable and even complimentary others were not. Many of the letters concerned the impact of a possible closing or of the S-U proposal. Others attack the administration for its softness toward students who were "obvious radicals or troublemakers." One letter signed by six different people included "We still favor our country over the Chicago 7 or Rubin who seems to be your peoples hero." A telegram read: "Stop Communistic take-over. Daughter sent to study Chemistry not Anarchy. Allow parents to vote on changes. We are paying the bill." An aftereffect of the events of May surfaced in June in the state legislature. The Ohio House passed a bill which provided for fines and jail sentences for any student, faculty, or staff involved in disruptions and for a one year dismissal if found guilty of breaking the law. Later in the month two legislators proposed an investigation of the New University at BG to see if its creation constituted a proper use of public funds. They referred to the curriculum of the New U. as "...new left propaganda, trivia, and subjects which could be handled in a simple lecture or debate." In spite of these aftershocks by the time school opened in the Fall the campus had returned to a state of relative, if anxious, calm.[44]

Epilogue and Prologue
The Jerome Years

On October 10, 1969 William T. Jerome in a letter to the Chair of the Board of Trustees, Donald G. Simmons, announced his resignation as President of the university. That the decision was not one of the moment is clear from a letter he wrote to Congressman Delbert L. Latta in January, 1969 in which he said that "...I am not actively involved in job hunting at this moment although I feel that my tenure at Bowling Green is approaching an end in the not too distant future." In his letter to the Board he asserted that the time was right for him to leave for there was at that point a happy conjuncture where "...his trust has been acquitted with some measure of success" and "...when the University itself is blessed with an aura of youthfulness, excitement, vitality, and promise which should make the post of president here attractive for my successor." Additionally, he saw that the years of growing enrollments and swelling budgets were approaching an end. The nature of the university in the 1970s was going to be perforce quite different, and he did not want to have to change his administrative style and expansive approach to meet the new realities. The Board accepted the resignation with regret and promised to expedite the search for a

successor. The following month a Presidential Search Committee was formed composed of fourteen members - five faculty,
four students, two trustees, one administrator, and two alumni.
This was the first presidential search in the history of the university to have students involved directly in the process. On May
13, 1970 at a special Board meeting the appointment of Hollis
A. Moore, Jr. as seventh president of Bowling Green State
University was announced.[45]

During June many tributes were made to President Jerome
for the seven years of leadership that he had given. The Faculty
Senate resolved in part:

> "Whether or not living is worth the time and effort is a question
> of quality. Better than any of us, Bill Jerome has understood
> this. And it is for the quality of life which he has brought to
> Bowling Green that we owe him our greatest debt. Although we
> can not measure this quality, we can, and hereby do, affirm
> it."[46]

As William T. Jerome III attended his last commencement as
President he could look back at a period of great change, excitement, and some disappointment, but as he told the Board he
was "...neither discouraged or dismayed." During his six years
much had transpired. Thirty-five million dollars in new construction had occurred, and there were 5000 more students and
two hundred more faculty than there had been in 1963. Some of
the changes had been dramatic such as an eight-story library and
an activist student body, while other alterations had been subtle
such as the transfer of the name Ad Building from one structure
to another and with that transfer of activity the disappearance
as a name and locale of "The Well" in the renamed University
Hall. In looking back over his administration President Jerome
felt his most important contributions had been the creation of
an awareness of the environment and of the cultural and
aesthetic aspects of life. In his closing remarks to the graduates
with his characteristic class, and maybe somewhat introspec-
tively, he said:

> "And when the winds of change blow, as well they will again
> and again, may you find them favorable, fresh, invigorating, a
> welcome aid as in the days of the great clipper ships in hastening
> you onward to your hearths, to your own havens, to your own
> special rendevous with life."[47]

As Hollis Moore assumed the presidency he was charged by the Board of Trustees to continue the work of his predecessor who had moved the university "...well on its way to becoming a great university."[48]

Notes

Chapter III

1. Seymour Martin Lipset, *The First New Nation: The United States in Historical and Comparative Perspective* (New York: W.W. Norton & Company, Inc., 1979), pp. VI, XII, and 124.

2. Linowitz, *Campus Tensions,* pp. 12-15.

3. *Ibid.,* p. 17.

4. *Ibid.,* p. 17.

5. *BGN,* Vol. 50, #160, April 27, 1966, p. 2.

6. *Ibid.,* Vol. 47, #29, Feb. 8, 1963, p.3, Vol. 49, #18, Nov. 24, 1964, p.3; Robert Moyers, ed., *First Bowling Green State University All-Sports Record Book 1974-75,* passim.

7. Gary E. Wilson, "The Historical Development of the Intramural Sports Program of Bowling Green State University" (unpublished Master's thesis, #3029, BGSU, 1976), pp. 110-120.

8. CAC. Fac. Sen. Coll., Box 10, Folder 1.

9. *Student Handbook - BGSU, 1963-64,* pp. 13-16; *New Student Handbook - BGSU, 1970, pp. 23-27; BGN,* Vol. 49, #28, Feb. 12, 1965, p. 1, Vol. 48, #41, March 27, 1964, p.1, #54, May 22, 1964, p. 1.

10. *BGN,* Vol. 49, #16, Nov. 17, 1964, p. 2, Vol. 51, #58, Feb. 7, 1967, p.5, #71, March 1, 1967, p. 4, #85, April 5, 1967, p. 5, & #95, April 21, 1967, p.5; *The Green Sheet,* Feb. 24-March 2, 1969.

11. *BOT. Min.* May 12, 1967.

12. *A WS Handbook 1963-64* and *1970. pp. 12-13 & 11; BGN,* Vol. 50, #100, April 27, 1966, p. 1, Vol. 51, #31, Nov. 10, 1966, p. 1, Vol. 53, #6, Oct. 3, 1968, p. 1, #20, Oct. 29, 1968, p. 1, #27, Nov. 11, 1968, p. 1, #47, Jan. 21, 1969, p. 4; Elsbrock, *Residence Life,* pp. 136-137; & *BOT Min,* Oct. 7, 1966.

13. *A WS,* 1963-64, p. 13 & *1970,* p. 11.

14. *BGN,* Vol. 52, #110, May 22, 1968, p. 1, Vol. 53, #73, March 6, 1969, pp. 1 & 12, #74, March 7, 1969, pp. 1 & 5, #75, March 11, 1969, pp. 1 & 2, #76, March 12, 1969, p. 2, and #77, March 13, 1969, p. 1.

15. Elsbrock, *Residence Life,* pp. 67, 102-103, & 113-115; *BGN,* Vol. 52, #19, Oct. 19, 1967, p. 1, #69, March 1, 1968, p. 1, #70, March 5, 1968, pp. 1 & 9, & #72, March 7, 1968, p.1.

16. *BOT Min,* March 4, 1966, Dec. 14, 1967, May 10, 1968, May 1, 1970, & July 10, 1970; *BGN,* Vol. 52, #58, Feb. 13, 1968, p. 1, #104, May 14, 1968, p. 1, Vol. 53, #50, Jan. 24, 1969, pp. 1 & 8, & #96, May 2, 1969, p. 1.

17. *A WS, 1963-64*pp. 12-23 & *1970,* pp. 10-17; *Bulletin.* 1963-64, p. 43, *1967-68,* pp. 53-54, *1971-72,* p. 37.

18. Elsbrock, *Residence Life,* pp. 133-35; *BGN,* Vol. 48, #12, Oct. 29, 1963, p.2, Vol. 51, #77, March 10, 1967, p. 1, #83, March 31, 1967, p. 1, #104, May 9, 1967, p. 6, Vol. 52, #32, Nov. 10, 1967, p. 1, Vol. 53, #51, Jan. 28, 1969, p. 1; *BOT Min,* Jan. 24, 1969, p. 1; *BGN,* Vol. 48, #43, Jan. 14, 1964, pp. 1 & 2, Vol. 54, #72, March 4, 1970, p. 2.

Notes

Chapter III (cont'd.)

19. *BGN*, Vol. 52, #12, Oct. 6, 1967, p. 1 (WTJ To Student Council), Vol. 53, #74, March 7, 1969, p. 5 (Al Baldwin, Student at Open Forum).

20. *Ibid.*, Vol. 49, #15, Nov. 13, 1964, p. 1, Vol. 50, #15, Oct. 14, 1965, p. 2, #64, Feb. 11, 1966, pp. 1 & 4, #65, Feb. 15, 1966, pp. 1 & 2, Vol. 51, #31, Nov. 10, 1966, p. 2, #61, Feb. 10, 1967, p. 1, Vol. 53, #66, Feb. 21, 1969, p. 1, #67, Feb. 25, 1969, p. 1, #69, Feb. 27, 1969, pp. 1 & 2, #70, Feb. 28, 1969, p. 1, #71, March 3, 1969, p. 1, #72, March 5, 1969, p. 6, #73, March 6, 1969, p. 1, #82, March 9, 1969, p.1, & #88, March 18, 1969, p. 1.

21. *Ibid.*, Vol. 49, #20, Dec. 8, 1964, p. 2, #21, Dec. 11, 1964, p. 2, #22, Dec. 15, 1964, p. 2, #32, Feb. 26, 1965, pp. 1 & 2, #36, March 12, 1965, p. 1, #55, May 28, 1965, p. 1, Vol. 53, #30, Nov. 14, 1968, p. 1, #31, Nov. 15, 1968, p. 1, #34, Nov. 21, 1968, p. 1, & #63, Feb. 18, 1969, p. 2.

22. Elsbrock, *Residence Life*, pp. 135-136; *BGN*, Vol. 48, #41, March 27, 1964, p. 1, Vol. 49, #28, Feb. 12, 1965, p. 1, Vol. 50, #102, April 29, 1966, p. 1, Vol. 51, #7, Sept. 29, 1966, p. 1., & Vol. 53, #75, March 12, 1969, p. 2.

23. *BOT Min.* December 14, 1967.

24. *BGN*, Vol. 51, #95, April 25, 1967, p. 1, #99, April 28, 1967, p. 1, Vol. 52, #1, Sept. 16, 1967, pp. 7-8, #8, Sept. 29, 1967, p. 1, #12, Oct. 6, 1967, p. 1, #16, Oct. 13, 1967, p. 21, Vol. 53, #11, Oct. 11, 1968, p. 1, #74, March 7, 1969, pp. 1 & 5, #75, March 11, 1969, pp. 1 & 2, #77, March 14, 1969, p. 2, #81, April 8, 1969, p. 1, #91, April 24, 1969, p. 2, #92, April 25, 1969, p. 1, #100, May 9, 1969, p. 1, #103, May 15, 1969, pp. 4 & 5, #111, May 29, 1969, pp. 5-8, Vol. 54, #17, Oct. 22, 1969, p. 1; Owens/Browne, *Teach-In*, pp. 64-69.

25. *BGN*, Vol. 53, #97, May 6, 1969, p. 2.

26. *Ibid.*, Vol. 54, #92, April 23, 1970, p. 1.

27. *Ibid.*, Vol. 54, #29, Nov. 11, 1969, p. 2, #92, April 23, 1970, p. 1, #93, April 24, 1969, p. 2; *Fac. Sen. Coll,* Box 10, Folder 3. WTJ, 2/3/70.

28. *BGN*, Vol. 49, #31, Feb. 23, 1965, p. 1, #32, Feb. 26, 1965, p. 1, #33, March 2, 1965, p. 2, Vol. 50, #59, Jan. 20, 1966, p. 1, #102, April 29, 1966, p. 1, Vol. 51, #46, Dec. 14, 1966, p. 1, #61, Feb. 10, 1967, p. 1, Vol. 53, #18, Oct. 24, 1968, p. 1, #54, Jan. 31, 1969, p. 5, Vol. 54, #40, Dec. 4, 1969, pp. 1-2, #42, Jan. 9, 1970, p. 1, #60, Feb. 10, 1970, pp. 1,4, & 5, #62, Feb. 12, 1970, p. 2, #63, Feb. 13, 1970, p. 1, #64, Feb. 17, 1970, pp. 1-2, #65, Feb. 18, 1970, p. 2, #90, April 21, 1970, pp. 1 & 3, #91, April 22, 1970, p. 1, & #92, April 23, 1970, pp. 1-2; *Fac. Sen. Coll,* Box 10, Folder 3, 4/21/70.

29. *BGN*, Vol. 53, #45, Jan. 16, 1968, p. 1, Vol. 54, #32, Nov. 14, 1969, p. 1, #44, Jan. 13, 1970, pp. 1-2; *BOT Min,* Jan. 9, 1970.

30. *BGN*, Vol. 53, #10, Oct. 10, 1968, p. 1, Vol. 54, #51, Jan. 23, 1970, p. 2, #87, April 15, 1970, p. 1. Vol. 51, #64, Feb. 16, 1967, p. 1, #84, April 4, 1967, p. 1, Vol. 53, #46, Jan. 17, 1969, p. 1, #47, Jan. 21, 1969, p. 1, #48, Jan. 22, 1969, p. 1, #49, Jan. 23, 1969, p. 1, & #50, Jan. 24, 1969, p. 1.

31. Linowitz, *Campus Tensions*, p. 53.

32. *BGN*, Vol. 48, #53, May 19, 1964, p. 2, #55, May 26, 1964, p. 2, Vol. 49, #5, Oct. 9, 1965, p. 1, Vol. 50, #1, Sept. 18, 1965, p. 12, #16, Oct. 15, 1965, p. 1,

Notes

Chapter III (cont'd.)
#29, Nov. 9, 1965, p. 1, Vol. 51, #4, Aug. 7, 1966, p. 1, #25, Nov. 1, 1966, p. 1, #26, Nov. 2, 1966, p. 1, #27, Nov. 3, 1966, p. 1, #28, Nov. 4, 1966, p. 2; *BOT Min.*, March 4, 1968.

33. *BGN*, Vol. 52, #73, March 8, 1968, p. 1, #100, May 7, 1968, pp. 1 & 5-7, Vol. 53, #20, Oct. 29, 1968, p. 1, #24, Nov. 5, 1968, p. 1, #27, Nov. 8, 1968, p. 1, #66, Feb. 21, 1969, p. 1, #67, Feb. 25, 1969, p. 2, #72, March 5, 1969, p. 1, #73, March 6, 1969, pp. 1 & 3, #74, March 7, 1969, p. 2, Vol. 54, #3, Sept. 25, 1969, p. 1, #17, Oct. 22, 1969, p. 1, #21, Oct. 29, 1969, p. 2, #96, May 1, 1970, p. 1, #97, May 5, 1970, p. 2; *BOT Min.* May 10, 1968.

34. *BGN*, Vol. 50, #18, Oct. 20, 1965, pp. 1, 2, & 6, #24, Oct. 29, 1965, p. 2, #28, Nov. 5, 1965, pp. 1 & 4, #30, Nov. 10, 1965, p. 2, #102, April 29, 1966, p. 1, Vol. 51, #90, April 13, 1967, p. 1, #92, April 18, 1967, p. 1, Vol. 52, #18, Oct. 18, 1967, p. 1, #19, Oct. 19, 1967, p. 2, #63, Feb. 21, 1968, p. 1, #66, Feb. 27, 1968, p. 5, #91, April 19, 1968, p. 1, Vol. 53, #20, Oct. 29, 1968, p. 1, #36, Nov. 26, 1968, p. 8, #37, Dec. 3, 1968, p. 1, #87, April 17, 1969, pp. 3-4, #89, April 22, 1969, p. 1, Vol. 54, #8, Oct. 3, 1969, p. 1, #10, Oct. 8, 1969, p. 1, #11, Oct. 14, 1969, pp. 2 & 8-9, #14, Oct. 16, 1969, pp. 1-2, #47, Jan. 16, 1970, p. 1, #49, Jan. 21, 1970, p. 1, #66, Feb. 20, 1970, p. 1, #88, April 16, 1970, p. 1, #103, May 14, 1970, p. 7, & #106, May 19, 1970, p. 4.

35. *Ibid.*, Vol. 54, #57, Feb. 4, 1970, p. 1, #74, March 6, 1970, p. 1, Vol. 54, #35, Nov. 20, 1969, p. 1, #38, Dec. 2, 1969, p. 1, #39, Dec. 3, 1969, p. 2, #55, Jan. 30, 1970, p. 2, #66, Feb. 19, 1970, p. 1, & #67, Feb. 20, 1970, p. 2.

36. *Ibid.*, Vol. 51, #33, Nov. 15, 1966, p. 1. (David George, Pres. of SDS); Owens/Browne, *Teach-In*, p. 48. (WTJ. III).

37. *BOT Min.*, July 22, 1965; *BGN*, Vol. 51, #23, Oct. 27, 1966, p. 2, #25, Nov. 1, 1966, p. 1, #26, Nov. 2, 1966, p. 2, #33, Nov. 15, 1966, p. 1, #35, Nov. 17, 1966, p. 1.

38. Owens/Browne, *Teach-In*, pp. 48-50; *BOT Min.*, May 10, 1968, Sept. 27, 1968, Oct. 10, 1969, May 1, 1970; *Fac. Sen. Coll,* Box 10, Folder 1, Oct. 15, 1968; *BGN*, Vol. 53, #2, Sept. 26, 1968, p. 1, #3, Sept. 27, 1968, p. 1, #4, Oct. 1, 1968, p. 1, #54, Jan. 31, 1969, p. 1, Vol. 54. #10, Oct. 8, 1969, p. 4, #13, Oct. 14, 1969, pp. 1-2, #77, March 12, 1970, p. 1, #92, April 23, 1970, p. 1.

39. *CAC-WTJ*, Box 8, Folder 2 (WTJ to B.M. Larrick, March 19, 1970), & Folder 1, (WTJ to J.P. Marino, March 19, 1970).

40. *Ibid.*, Folder 1, June 1969; *BOT Min.*, Oct. 10, 1969, March 6, 1970; *BGN*, Vol. 53, #89, April 22, 1969, p. 2, Vol. 54, #12, Oct. 10, 1969, p. 2, #70, Feb. 27, 1970, pp. 1-2, & #71, March 3, 1970, p. 2.

41. *Fac. Sen. Coll*, Box 10, Folder 3. (Letter from WTJ to Joseph K. Balogh, Chair of Faculty Senate).

42. *Ibid.*, (Senate Minutes); Owens/Browne, *Teach-In*, pp. 26-33; *BGN*, Vol. 54, #89, April 17, 1970, p. 1, #92, April 23, 1970, p. 1, #94, April 28, 1970, p. 5, #96, May 1, 1970, p. 1, #97, May 5, 1970, pp. 1-2 & 4-5, #98, May 6, 1970, p. 2, #99, May 7, 1970, p. 1, #100, May 8, 1970, p. 1, #101, May 12, 1970, p. 2, #103, May 14, 1970, pp. 4-5, #105, May 18, 1970, pp. 1-3, #108, May 21, 1970, p. 1.

43. Owens/Browne, *Teach-In*, pp. 130 & 142; *BOT Min.*, May 13, 1970.

Notes

Chapter III (cont'd.)

44. *CAC-WTJ*, Box 10, Folder 18; *BGN*, Vol. 54, #115, June 3, 1970, p. 1, #116, June 4, 1970, p. 1, & Vol. 55, #16, Sept. 29, 1970, p. 1.

45. *BOT Min.*, Oct. 10, 1969 & May 13, 1970; *CAC-WTJ*, Box 31, Folder 5; CAC-75th Anniversary Tapes. Interview with W.T.J. on Nov. 11, 1985; *BGN*, Vol. 54, #13, Oct. 14, 1969, p. 1, #34, Nov. 19, 1969, p. 1, & #35, Nov. 20, 1969, p. 2.

46. *Fac. Sen. Coll,* Box 10, Folder 3. (Minutes of June 2, 1970).

47. *BGN*, Vol. 54, #117, June 5, 1970, p. 5; *CAC-WTJ*, Box 29, Folder 17, "The Winds of Change", p. 6.

48. *BOT. Min.*, Oct. 10, 1969.

SECTION III
"A DECADE OF DISTINCTION"
The Moore Administration
1970-1981

Hollis A. Moore, Jr.
President — 1970-1981

86

CHAPTER IV

THE STEADY STATE INSTITUTION
The Campus, Its Programs, and Its People

Building in the 1970s — Offenhauer Towers

The Student Recreation Center Opening — 1978

CHAPTER IV

THE STEADY STATE INSTITUTION
The Campus, Its Programs, and Its People

The appointment of Hollis A. Moore, Jr. as the seventh President of Bowling Green State University was announced on May 13, 1970 just following one of the most tense periods in the history of the university. He stated at the time that the manner in which Bowling Green had conducted itself during the first two weeks of May gave him much encouragement for the continued well-being of the institution.

Hollis A. Moore's academic and professional background was similar in many ways to four of the first six presidents. He came from a public education experience with his most recent position being that of Vice President for Academic Affairs at George Peabody College — a school noted for its training of educators. Like the more recent presidents he was not a Buckeye by either birth or experience. At age forty seven he brought both skills and enthusiasm to the campus.

Moore became President at a time when public confidence in institutions and their managers was at a nadir. Ten years later when asked what the greatest challenge facing him was as he assumed office he replied to "stimulate confidence in univ (sic) on part of *all* constituencies." He took up the task of President fully aware that the times were uncertain and that the future held a clear slowing down of the type of growth that had marked the preceding twenty years.[1]

A Philosophy and An Aim

"Mindful of this university's rich tradition, but convinced that its greatest days are yet to be,"[2]

Entering office at a time of crisis but convinced that the 70s would be "a decade of distinction," President Moore in his early statements dealt with both situations. On such immediate concerns as university governance reorganization, teacher evaluation, and the New U he indicated the need for caution, but not necessarily rejection. As school opened in September he expressed his feelings about the climate of the nation, thusly: "Too many Americans, young and old, are becoming an unsmiling people, filled with resentments, weighted down with causes of the right or left, and taking themselves and their crusades so seriously that many of us have become sententious bores or dangerous purveyors of hate."[3]

Over the decade some themes continued constant, but substantially changing conditions dictated alterations in emphasis and some policies. In his first speeches to faculty and students President Moore stressed that Bowling Green must continue to provide excellence in the classroom and quality experiences extramurally. This entailed a broad liberal education for all, an increased interdisciplinary approach to teaching, an improved freshman experience, better residence hall programming, and greater exposure to other cultures. To accomplish this he asserted that the divisions of the 1960s and the ruptures of the past Spring must be replaced by agreement and solidarity among all segments of the university community. At the President's Convocation, in the Spring of 1971, Moore's low-key inauguration, he accentuated that Bowling Green was both a state university on the one hand and an institution of higher learning on the other, and consequently must serve but also seek. These twin goals of practicality and liberality became the bench marks used for implementing educational programs during the 1970s although they did not bring the wished for solidarity. As early as the second year of his administration a new and what proved to be an increasingly nagging element entered the scene; namely, a worsening state and national financial crunch. Fluctuations occurred during the remainder of the decade, and even though federal funding improved, support from the state was often unreliable. These fiscal developments lead President Moore increasingly to emphasize the need for "creative responses" to financing and to institute better resource planning. As the 70s elapsed finances came to so dominate Moore's concern for the university that in 1980 he declared that the greatest challenge facing Bowling Green was to "...retain solvency — continue vitality and renewal."

As the 1980s approached President Moore began planning for the next decade. In a speech entitled "Leadership: The Presidential Imperative" he listed five obligations of leadership for the 1980s. They were: 1) sustain vitality of the institution, 2) follow fairness and equity in decision making, 3) preserve quality against all hardship and change, 4) understand and use symbolic behavior, and 5) avoid short term solutions to long term problems. In a later speech he added that Bowling Green needed to seek excellence more than uniqueness and enhance the areas where distinction exists and cut involvement in those where it does not. In his last address to the faculty President Moore hit on one other need for the 80s—that of greater coordination and cooperation between higher education and public education. He argued that there was a need for improvement at both levels, and predicted that if the two instrumentalities did not test and improve their product it would be done for them.[4]

All's Not Bricks and Mortar

"It was clear to me when I took the position that the president of a university in the 1970's would have his name on a minimal number of plaques."[5]

While the twenty years prior to the Moore administration had been ones of great growth, the period 1970 to 1981 saw state support for capital improvements decline and actually cease between 1977 and 1981. During that decade Bowling Green received the least capital money of any of the twelve state universities The dearth of support occasionally was especially frustrating, such as in 1974 when President Moore told the faculty that "The State of Ohio announced the construction of restrooms on I-75 between Bowling Green and Findlay planned to cost $2,579,403.15, a third of a million dollars more than the total capital appropriation for this university since 1971. This tells us something about the relative status of colleges and comfort stations."[6] Even so, during Moore's presidency twelve major and three minor buildings were either planned, built, or completed.

The practice started in the 1960s by the Ohio Board of Regents to receive biennial capital improvement requests was continued through the 1970s. Bowling Green, therefore, submitted every two years prioritized rolling projections for the next six years. The requests reflected both a wish list and projects that were thought at the time to be needed. Over the decade projects appeared on the list with a high priority only to disappear later or never be funded. Among those proposed were a new Social Sciences Classroom building, a relocated Health and Physical Education Center, a Continuing Education Center, an Instructional Media Center and Language Laboratory, a Center for International Studies, additions to Memorial Hall and IET, and major renovation to Hanna, Hayes, and Moseley Halls. Interestingly in regard to renovation two of the three buildings just listed, Hanna and Moseley, in 1973 were recommended by an architecural consultant to be replaced rather than refurbished.[7]

Funded construction in the 70s was quite diverse running from new buildings to renovation and refurbishing to safety additions. In the early years of the Moore administration four buildings planned and/or begun under Jerome were completed; namely, Offenhauer East and West, the Technology Building, The Business Administration Building, and Firelands North Building. Just two academic buildings were planned and built under President Moore — the College of Musical Arts Center which opened in 1979 and the 1980 exercise building built on the site of the former Natatorium. Two special use structures were planned and built both of which were criticized by the *BG News*, but became highly acclaimed in time. In 1974 the Alumni Association announced an $800,000 fund raising campaign in order to construct an Alumni Center. The *News* editorially attack the plan as wasteful arguing that the money could better be spent other ways at the university. The campaign continued with considerable success and in 1976 the Alumni Center was opened. The same year that the Alumni drive began, President Moore indicated the need for a new swimming facility to which the *News* responded: "New aquatic center; you must be kidding! The idea is nothing more than a pipedream and a ploy to channel even more money into an already stuffed athletic budget.''[8] Two years later after much study and surveying of student opinion approval was given for the planning and construction of a special fee-financed Student Recreation Center. The views expressed by the *BG News* concerning intercollegiate athletics did reflect those held by many students and eventuated in a building dedicated to general student recreational use almost exclusively. The only exception to that policy regarded swimming where both instructional and intercollegiate use was permitted. This was fully legitimatized in 1982 when the state assumed the cost of the aquatic portion of the building on the grounds of its academic usage. An assortment of other buildings appeared, the chief among them being a new warehouse, a green house for campus plants, a new entrance road and information center at the east entrance to the university, and the reconstruction of a one room school house adjacent to the Education Building which became known as the Educational Memorabilia Center.[9]

A largely new development of the 1970s that carried on into the 80s was that of refurbishing and renovating older buildings. On several occasions during the decade the large and small residence halls were given major overhauls, a development that President Moore credited with helping to maintain student desire to live on campus. The three oldest academic buildings were all worked on with new energy efficient windows being installed and retucking and waterproofing of the exterior bricks. In 1973 and in 1975 two theatre renovations resulted in a completely remodeled Main Auditorium followed by the conversion of 105 Hanna Hall into a film theatre which in 1976 was named the Dorothy and Lillian Gish Film Theatre honoring two early movie stars who were Ohio natives. The largest renovation was that of the old library or Graduate Center which underwent a major reconstruction in 1976-1977 into offices for the President and Provost, the Graduate College, the Undergraduate Admission office, the Faculty Senate, and offices for Continuing Education plus a meeting room and an art gallery. This building with Board approval was renamed in 1976 the Kenneth H. McFall Center in honor of Vice President Emeritus McFall. As new construction faded and renovation grew a greater appreciation for the maintenance of the physical plant arose. In 1974

President Moore commissioned F.E. Beatty, Director of Buildings and Facilities, "...to organize, direct, and conduct an extensive inventory of the physical condition of each of the existing buildings and to forecast the needs for the ensuing years."[10] This resulted in the issuance in 1975 of the *Bowling Green State University Capital Expenditure Requirements For Existing Buildings 1975-1995* which provided an inventory of maintenance needs and costs."[11]

A variety of other acquisitions, modifications, and construction happened that improved the university's physical plant. In lieu of a new building for the School of Art a former factory on East Reed Street was acquired in 1971, and became the Art Annex housing studios for such areas as ceramics, glass, and sculpturing. The same year a cottage on sorority row with the aid of a grant by Dr. Paul D. Wurzburger was converted into a French speaking house, and was dedicated by the French Ambassador to the United States as La Maison Francaise. The raised awareness of the human and environmental atmosphere mandated a number of changes. These ranged from the installation in 1974 of smoke and heat detectors in residence halls, to a self-contained air-conditioning system for the Drosophila Center, to a separate chemical storage building. Late in the Moore administration plans for a separate animal laboratory annex were developed, but financing proved difficult with the result that it was not started until after his death. One other health concern, the presence of asbestos, emerged in the 1970s, but had its primary impact in the 80s. While not a health concern, federal and state regulations and funding propelled the university, starting in 1974, toward making the campus as barrier free as possible. The process was a continuing one that began with the construction of ramps and the cutting of curbs and moved on to the installation of automatic doors and elevators.[12]

A corollary but special environmental problem plagued the university throughout the 70s. The general issue was the disposal of waste with the most acute aspect being air pollution. The largest source of air soiling was the central heating plant which poured out excessive amounts of sulphur dioxide particulates. In 1971 the decision was made to convert the plant from coal to gas or oil. With state financial support the project was undertaken but in the late stages of completion the oil and then the gas shortages hit forcing a return to complete reliance on coal. In 1977 the federal EPA notified the university that it had until October of 1979 to clean up its smokestack emissions. The following year the Board of Regents and the Ohio EPA agreed to fund at one million dollars the installation of an electrostatic precipatator. In February 1980 the final test on the new system was run and after a decade or more it was announced that Bowling Green was within the legal particulate tolerances allowed by federal law. Also during the 1970s several of the then forty four incinerators had afterburners attached to them while the rest of them were shut down, and the trash was disposed of as solid waste at a landfill.[13]

Auxiliary and special facilities are an important part of any campus, and often in time even become an integral part of it. The major expansion of athletic and recreational facilities occurred in the 60s but some additions and minor honing continued with more tennis courts in 1971, the expansion in 1973-74 of the golf course to eighteen holes, the lighting of the intramural fields east of Yount Road, and the construction in 1975 of an athletic storage building adjacent to Whittaker Track.[14] The 70s witnessed a significant increase in the power and scope of WBGU-TV. In 1971, Channel 57 which had been reserved for Lima was reallocated to WBGU-TV as part of a new state wide educational network. To serve the new enlarged market of northwest Ohio, a transmitter was erected near Deshler and the station output was increased to 30,000 watts. Transmission commenced in 1973. Five years later the Corporation for Public Broadcasting financed the cost of a satellite receiving dish which was built near the campus station. During 1979 discussions that proved abortive were held with the Toledo PBS station in what was hoped might be a money saving cooperative effort or even consolidation. By 1980 the original studio building was too small to serve its functions and those of its cohort the Northwest Ohio Educational Television Foundation. Therefore, arrangements were made which permitted the construction of an addition to the station to handle the administrative aspects of the educational programming.[15]

Computers and their usage followed a similar pattern of growth and efforts at cooperation. President Moore discovered in 1970 that the budget for computational services had risen from $160,000 in 1967-68 to an estimated $549,000. The cost and the impetus from OBOR for regional cooperation led Bowling Green to pursue with the University of Toledo the possibilities. After some difficulty the way was paved through the efforts of Owens-Illinois which provided land at its Levis Development Park and some financial incentives for the creation of what became the J. Preston Levis Regional Computer Center. In 1978 the City of Toledo and a regional planning unit joined the consortium. At approximately that point problems appeared in providing the university with the needed academic and administrative services it expected and was paying for. During the last three years of the Moore administration moves toward disengagement occurred, but a complete break did not come until later.[16]

The needs of the city and the university over the years have been dealt with cooperatively. Such remained the case during the 70s. In 1970 the university deeded land to the city that made it possible to widen Thurstin Street between Ridge and Wooster and to align it with Manville Avenue on the south; all of which was mutually beneficial. The next year the city was granted an easement along Poe Road so the city could construct a sanitary sewer. While there were health and esthetic benefits gained from this project, a certain air about Bowling Green was lost except to folklore by its completion. The opening of I-75 and the subsequent commercial development along East Wooster made of it a congested thoroughfare. In 1975 the university again agreed to cooperate in ceding land that would enable Wooster to be widened. One other cooperative venture centered around the development of the Sterling Farm area with the construction of the Musical Arts and Student Recreation buildings. In order to service the structures and to provide parking better access was needed. Consequently in 1979-1980 East Merry Street was extended from Willard Street to Yount Road.[17]

If building did not keep pace with the 1960s the naming of structures and facilities did. In 1971 the twin tower residence hall that had been planned and erected using the name

McDonald Addition was designated by the Board of Trustees as Offenhauer Towers East and West in honor of the university's second President, Roy E. Offenhauer. During the course of the decade four other individuals were honored in a similar way. In 1976 Nick J. Mileti, an enthusiastic and supportive alumnus, was recognized when the Alumni Center was given his name. In 1981 the other three individuals were commended. In March the Board named the physical education units, North Gym (Women's Gym) and South Gym (Men's Gym) and the new exercise building, the Eppler Complex in honor of the former longtime head of the women's physical education program, Gertrude Eppler. In May the Board designated the Musical Arts Center as the Hollis and Marian Moore Musical Arts Center. The commemoration was in recognition of President Moore's eleven years of service and of the role that he and Marian Moore had played in procuring the private funding of the performance areas of the new building. Four of the most significant of the private contributors had been recognized earlier when the auditorium was named the Lenore and Marvin Kobacker Hall and the smaller facility the Dorothy and Ashel Bryan Recital Hall. While not new, the appellation of specific facilities and rooms for largely former faculty and staff markedly increased in the latter 1970s and into the 1980s. Among those so honored were: Willard E. Singer—a lecture hall; Leon L. Winslow, Earl C. Powell, Daniel J. Crowley, and Roland C. Torgerson— seminar rooms; Samuel M. Cooper—swimming pool; Agnes M. Hooley—conference room; Robert J. Keefe—tennis courts; and Cornelius Cochran—soccer field.

Little Is Ever New
Variations on University Governance

"...I will seek consensus, but not at the price of progress; in our deliberations I will ask for your cooperation, never your capitulation;"[19]

During his term as President Hollis Moore made relatively few speeches to the university community concerning his views on management. The best insights came from presentations he made to outside groups. In the Spring of 1973 in a speech to the

Bellevue Chamber of Commerce his ideas were thoroughly elucidated. He asserted that the 1970s demanded a new approach and continued on saying that:

> "...the problems of adjustment are more difficult in colleges and universities than in most other organizations because they have been undermanaged, especially at the departmental level.
>
> The process of adjustment is not moving fast enough; on some campuses there is still more concern with prestige than with flexibility; expansionist tendencies are still evident; some faculty members seem to view the present situation as merely a temporary aberration from the 'golden years' pattern.
>
> During the 'golden years' leadership was seen as mediating conflicts between ambitious campus departments. During the recent period of campus disturbances, leadership was identified with keeping the peace. Now, in contrast to that recent past, leadership will be identified in the context of educational policy making and resource planning. On campus and off it will be identified through the choices it makes."[20]

Four years later in another non-university speech he averred that a major challenge was "How to maintain vitality and creative change despite static enrollment, stable faculty size, and inadequate state tax resources."[21]

In order to accomplish his goals President Moore set about revamping the administrative organizational pattern. The primary aim was to place all academic and student functions under the direction of the Provost—the title Vice President for Academic Affairs was dropped. Under the leadership of the Provost were initally four Vice Provosts responsible for Faculty Affairs, Student Affairs, Research and Graduate Studies, and Continuing Education. Additionally, there were Vice Presidents for Operations, Public Service, and for general administrative and Board of Trustee affairs. In keeping with his concern about resource planning, Moore created the new position of Coordinator for Planning and Budgeting. The whole plan was geared to organize by function the university administration, and in the process lessen from the Jerome model the number of administrators reporting directly to the President.

Over the period of the first two years of the Moore administration, as the reorganization occurred, there was a complete turnover of the top administrative personnel. All three of the Vice Presidents appointed by Jerome left Bowling Green, interestingly to assume a presidency either immediately or within a relatively short period — B.D. Owens at the University of Tampa, James Bond at California State College at Sacramento, and Stanley Coffman at SUNY-New Paltz. The new administrative team created by President Moore was composed of young and creative individuals, a number of whom were relatively inexperienced. Of that original group two became stalwarts—Richard A. Edwards and Michael R. Ferrari—while most of the rest either did not work out or left for other positions. Two other individuals who emerged to positions of importance where they remained for the duration of the Moore years were James E. Hof in alumni affairs, public service, and development and Richard R. Eakin in student affairs and institutional planning. One major new administrative area was fashioned to deal both with university commitments made for the development of minority enrollment and to meet increased federal laws and directives concerning civil rights. While support personnel had been added starting in 1968 it was not until 1974, when Charles L. Means was hired, that a top administrator was given sole responsibility for the whole gamut of minority affairs.[22]

At the time of crisis in May 1970 there was considerable sentiment among students that the proper, and possibly only, solution to university governance was the creation of a community council/assembly or some form of a unicameral representative body. Momentum for a change was considerable when Hollis Moore assumed the presidency—a task force having been named by Jerome to "...study and recommend the approach Bowling Green should consider to provide participation and communication of all segments...in the governance of our university."[23] The task force report in the Fall of 1970 suggested two possible approaches; namely, a Model A which was a Community Council/University Assembly alternative or a Model B which proposed a University Senate option. Neither the Faculty Senate or President Moore liked the proposals and so a second group, the Charter Commission, was appointed in April, 1971 to develop an alternative to Model A. The Commission late in the year submitted its idea — a council-assembly form of government. The 1972-73 school year found the Faculty Senate studying the Charter, but ignoring the Charter Commission Report. In February 1973 President Moore indicated his dislike of the university assembly approach and in May named yet another body, The Committee on University Governance and Reorganization (COUGAR), chaired by Peter Facione. The committee was charged "...to conduct a complete examination of our University's organizational structures and governance systems..." The final output of COUGAR was a document entitled "The Academic Charter" which though modified by both Faculty Senate and the Board of Trustees was finally approved by the Board in September 1976. The new charter did not dramatically revise the older Faculty Charter, but did broaden it to include and/or recommend student representation on most university, college, and department policy committees. The new charter reflected the attitudes of many faculty and of President Moore who believed in a cooperative check and balance system and the value of student involvement.

While the efforts to forge a new form of governance went on a group initially of Arts and Science College departmental chairs formed an ad hoc organization that they called the Council of Chairs. By the Fall of 1972 it had become a university-wide body representing the views of the Chairs and ostensibly the departments. The Council grew in influence although it was never officially recognized. Three years following the adoption of the Academic Charter a further refinement to university governance was made. While not included in the Charter either, President Moore in 1979 reactivated a former advisory body to the Administration for classified employees which he named the Personnel Steering Committee.[23]

Venturesomeness - Goals and Achievements

"Wisdom, sound judgment, tolerance, and respect for other persons, cultures, and ideas are the hallmarks of an educated person and the characteristics which BGSU hopes to develop in its students."[24]

The foregoing, a part of the revised statement of academic goals of 1978, reflected a key portion of the educational philosophy of the 1970s. However, it was only half of the picture. While President Moore continually emphasized the importance of a liberal education, especially of an interdisciplinary nature, he also stressed the university's responsibility to serve the vocational needs of the students and the manpower requirements of society. He hoped that the university would be able to accomodate these demands by developing various academic solutions. To this end Moore encouraged and directed the launching of what he called a "feisty" approach. Yet, the university did not completely control its own direction.

From its creation in 1963 the Ohio Board of Regents became an external force which influenced, modified, and upon occasion dictated policy that effected universities. Twice during the 70s the Regents issued master plans for higher education in Ohio. The first known as the Warren-King Report appeared shortly before Hollis Moore assumed office. While it contained numerous ideas the most significant for Bowling Green was that of an enrollment limit. Both Jerome before he left and Moore as he arrived recognized the potential inhibiting influence on curricular growth of such a freeze. In 1975 the next plan stressed the elimination of barriers that limited access to higher education, called for more emphasis and resources to be placed on lifelong learning, advocated maintaining and rewarding quality teaching and research, and supported the training of individuals in the area of health care. There were no objections to these goals, but they entailed money which was in short supply. The Ohio Board of Education late in 1974 mandated a complete redesign of teacher education to be in place by 1980. Finally, the federal government also exerted influences especially in the areas of civil and equal rights that impacted the academic offerings and the student mix significantly.[26]

During the last year of the Jerome administration considerable movement began toward reconsideration and innovation in both curriculum and pedagogy. This was first evidenced in *The White Paper* and then practically experimented with, although under some duress, in the New University of the Spring of 1970. The New U experiment carried over to the Fall when some fifteen courses were offered in the five "colleges" of Minority Studies, Peace, Community Relations, Culture, and Ecology. While the primary value of the New U was political and psychological, it did help emphasize that there was faculty and student interest in new and what were considered more meaningful approaches to learning. The stimulus for change having occurred, the next few years witnessed debate, experimentation, disappointment, and change.[27]

In addition to the informal New U offerings the Fall of 1970 also saw the transformation of the Honors Program into an Experimental Studies Program which broadened its availability to students interested in independent study. Additionally, the First Little College began with ninety students and four faculty in a course entitled "The Making and Manipulation of Images." The Little College was aimed at exposing students to the interdisciplinary nature of learning in a small, personalized form of instruction while fostering both critical thinking and individual value systems. A further approach to an integrated curriculum was initiated in 1971-72 in the form of the Cluster College; a one quarter "living-learning" experience. During the year a Humanities and a Physical Sciences cluster were offered, both of which stressed the multidisciplinary nature of learning and the interrelationship of all aspects of college life. The predominant theme of these various approaches was the improvement of general education. President Moore advocated early in his administration the creation of a School of Introductory Studies and also the development of a time-shortened baccalaureate degree program. A major breakthrough happened in 1972 when The Carnegie Foundation granted $142,000 to support the development of a Modular Achievement Program which was designed to "define achievement criteria and select appropriate evaluation instruments to measure performance." The goal of MAP was to offer an integrated program of study which for those who mastered it could lead to the telescoping of the requirements of the first two years. One other path made available was opened with the creation of the degree of Bachelor of Liberal Studies which permitted a largely self designed degree program.[28]

While various options for students appeared, planning and debate about further possibilities continued. In 1972 the College of Arts and Sciences formed a Curriculum Revision Committee to review primarily the general education and group requirement offerings of the College. In its recommendations the committee called for an integrated approach to the various group requirements and for developing in all disciplines introductory courses for the non-major. In 1971 and in 1972, in the hope that ideas could be shared and excitement generated among the faculty, conferences were held on the topics of innovative teaching and the teaching of values. Two university wide committees were created in January 1972 charged to study and make recommendations on 1) a redefined baccalaureate and 2) introductory studies. Their reports a year later called for the greater use of evaluative examinations for placement and credit, the streamlining and coordination of general education, greater flexibility of scheduling, better advising, the increased use of the Little and Cluster Colleges, and some small classes for all freshmen. Despite the great emphasis on reform at the underclass level a quite different concern arose in the early 70s. The demand for teachers began to decline and opportunities in business were uncertain, all of which posed a question as to the suitability of the curriculum. President Moore formed a "Blue Ribbon" committee to study the situation. In the Spring of 1971 it urged the reconsideration of the curriculum so as to offer training in areas that would serve "society's future needs." Among the areas suggested were health and social services, environmental control, industrial technology, and recreation. At the same time the Academic Council created the Academic Development and Evaluation Committee System (ADEC) which in Moore's words provided "...the mechanism for allowing the university to function in a state of perpetual transformation while recognizing, not the appropriateness of change for the sake of change, but rather the inappropriateness of maintaining a static system in a world in which change for the sake of survival is seen as mandatory."[29]

The above recommendations and planning modes led to further curricular and institutional alterations. In 1973 in an effort to meet the changing job market the first college to be created in thirty eight years—the College of Health and Community Services—was formed. It was viewed as a vehicle to train technical people for positions in the rapidly expanding health and social services fields. Two years later in a similar vein the College of Musical Arts and the School of Speech Communications were created, and the Department of Nursing was moved from Arts and Sciences into the College of Health and Community Services as a school. In the intervening year, 1974, the success of MAP and further planning led to a major grant of $500,000 from the Fund for Improvement of Postsecondary Education (FIPSE) to support the creation and functioning of a Competency-based Undergraduate Education Center (CUE Center). The Center which opened in the Fall of 1974 saw its overall mission as helping discover... "more about generic competencies (skills, capabilities, knowledges, behaviors) that general education has, implicitly at least, always sought but never been pressed to define and defend."[30] To accomplish its goal the Center encouraged and aided faculty in defining and researching core competencies, carried on research by its staff, and developed for local and national use a bibliographic information service on competency-based education.[31]

By 1975-76 most of the more experimental approaches had been initiated and some were being modified while still others had run their course. One perennial proposed modification that ran through the whole decade of the 70s and into the 80s was that of calendar reform. President Moore starting in 1971 advocated an "early out" calendar for pedagogical, job opportunity related, and campus stability reasons. Consequently several committees, both administrative and faculty, studied, debated, and recommended during the period with no real agreement being reached. The early discussion centered around starting school early and splitting the Winter Quarter in half around the Christmas break. Late in the 70s when the Board of Regents agreed to allow schools to opt for an early semester calendar that idea became the center of debate. In general the student body opposed change and the faculty split rather evenly while the administration favored it.[32]

Concern over calendar reform was only one aspect of faculty resistance to some of the curricular reshaping of the early 1970s. In the Spring of 1972 a report from a committee established to consider a program of introductory studies raised one of the basic questions that worried faculty. In referring to an evaluation of the Little College the committee said that what the students "...learned seemed to be more in the area of self-realization and understanding, rather than course content."[33] A year later this theme and others were proclaimed in a position paper issued by thirty members of the Psychology Department. They argued that the university was not a job-training center or an institution primarily concerned with growth potential. They also attacked the position that a subject must be "relevant" to be meaningful. The essence of the paper was that a university was unique because of "...its devotion to excellence in the creation, examination, and dissemination of knowledge."[34] The Psychology position was not universally accepted and the debate continued over what the true role of introductory courses should be.

While precise agreement on the academic goals of the university did not emerge, a consensus did occur on the need to evaluate both experimental programs and normal ongoing curricular developments. This agreement evolved in the form of the already mentioned planning committee, ADEC, and in the Fall of 1974 of the Committee on Program Evaluation (COPE). The latter was a part of the Academic Council and was charged with the responsibility "...to formulate guidelines for departmental and unit self-study, to work with departments and units in completing reports and to coordinate the over-all process."[35] The plan when in place provided for a revue of all academic programs every five years. In 1980 in line with OBOR pressures the system was reorganized and emerged as the Program for Academic Review and Evaluation.[36]

Even though the supporters of experimentation and curricular reform disagreed with the basic premises of their critics, they recognized that their goals had not been entirely gained. In his summary report in 1978 as he left office, Provost Kenneth Rothe stated that "...even a modicum of honesty requries us to admit that neither our general studies program nor the vast majority of such programs nationally has succeeded in producing the breadth of knowledge or honing of the intellect sought, let alone guaranteed the lesser skills attainment such as reading, writing and basic mathematics."[37] Acceptance of these short-comings had as early as 1974 generated a move toward centralization of control and discussion of university wide general education goals.

In May 1974 the Academic Council approved creation of the University Division of General Studies with a charge to administer all general education courses and to counsel underclass students who had not declared a major. As the decade passed the University Division came to also coordinate inter-disciplinary, innovative, and experimental courses for freshmen and sophomores and to administer such varied programs as MAP, Coordinated Quarters, Little College, Cluster College, and Advanced Placement and Accelerated Programs. In 1980 the Center for Educational Options was created to administer the various special programs just mentioned plus the newly revived honors program. The University Division was placed under the College of Arts and Sciences and assigned the sole responsibility of operating the General Education Program. President Moore in his speech to the faculty in September 1977 referred to a decline in SAT scores and asserted that "We attach the most central importance to restoring the traditions of critical reading and careful writing."[38] This assertion reenforced the efforts already under way to construct a general studies curriculum. During the same Fall the Academic Council approved a statement of goals which emphasized that students should be skilled in logical thinking and problem solving, reading and writing, computation, speaking and listening, and decision making and values conflict clarification. A year later the Council endorsed a revised set of ten educational goals which were divided into five essential skills and five areas of functional understanding. The skills were those of 1977 and the functional understandings were literature, fine arts and humanities, natural sciences and technology, social and behavioral sciences, and foreign cultures and personal development; the latter five reflected the political fine tuning of the process. Ironically, just as the general studies agreements were being reached there emerged the national awareness that the development of critical skills was as much a K through twelve problem as it was a university one. Consequently, in the early 1980s Bowling Green and its sister institutions along with public school authorities began attacking that problem.[39]

During the 1970s ethnocentricity in the curriculum was appreciably modified by an upsurge of interest in other groups and cultures. The change in approach came from a multitude of causes — genuine academic interest, student pressures and demands, and general national awareness. Prior to the arrival of President Moore the university had begun to emphasize the importance of international education; a position he strongly supported. As a result in the early 70s there emerged a number of area study programs such as Asian, Latin American, and Russian plus the development of student teaching opportunities in South America and Quebec. The major thrust of the decade came, however, in Afro-American and Latino studies. The demands of Black students in the Spring of 1970 led to the development of both increased efforts to attract minority students and the offering of courses dealing with minority culture and experiences. Immediately following the crisis of early May, 1970 the university began an active recruiting effort and established a program, the Student Development Program, to help students academically and financially. Within one college generation minority enrollment had increased five fold, the overall quality of the students had improved, and the retention rate had increased. The process was not without controversy and cost nor was it always viewed as being enough, but progress was made. In the early 70s courses dealing with Blacks and Black themes were instituted, and by 1972 an Afro-American Studies major had evolved along with an Ethnic Studies Center. During the course of the decade a faculty evolved that taught courses primarily in Black and Latino areas. By 1979 the faculty and courses had gradually coalesced into the Department of Ethnic Studies. While greater headway was made with Black recruitment and studies, efforts were made to reproduce a similar program for Hispanics, which only began to succeed in the early 1980s.

The growing social awareness of the role of women in modern society helped lead in the Spring of 1971 to the first women's study course which was entitled "Problems and Potentials of Women I." Gradually from that point other courses began to be offered so that by the Fall of 1976 a general enough pattern of courses generating student interest had developed to warrant a request for the establishment of a formal Women's Studies Program. The Academic Council approved the request and by the beginning of the 1978-79 academic year a program was well established.[40]

While Bowling Green during the 1970s experienced little growth in enrollment and was confronted by financial constrictions a great deal of academic and managerial creativity was attempted. As already seen, some of the efforts succeeded and others did not. This spirit of experimentation became a hall mark of the Moore administration even though often marred by frustration and failure. President Moore was attracted to ideas and creativeness and to people who seemed to embody those traits. He was proud of "appointing a 32-year-old wavemaker from Penn as Provost" and "establish(ing) a resource planning team under a 32-year-old management expert."[41] Other young individuals were appointed to various positions in his quest for creative and imaginative academic growth. Moore's initiative coupled with that of his administrative team and much of the faculty did result in considerable curricular and organizational development. As previously noted a new college, that of Health and Community Services, was created which over the decade began offering programs in social work, criminal justice, child and family services, gerontology, medical records administration, applied microbiology, dietetics, environmental health, medical technology, parisitology and medical entomology, physical therapy, and speech pathology and audiology. The newly renamed College of Arts and Sciences introduced programs and degrees in such areas as film studies, creative writing, astronomy, environmental science, and communications. New programs in the College of Business appeared in public and institutional administration, industrial and labor relations, and health care administration.[42]

Another reflection of the internal dynamism of change was the academic reorganization that occurred. In addition to the two new colleges and the School of Nursing there emerged during the 70s also the School of Speech Communication, School of Technology, and School of Health, Physical Education, and

Recreation (HPER). Within the older colleges some new and some reorganized departments evolved as well. In Arts and Sciences departments of Popular Culture and Ethnic Studies were created and two departments expanded their mission and thus names; Mathematics to Mathematics and Statistics and Physics to Physics and Astronomy. In Business the Department of Business Law was renamed the Department of Legal Studies, while the Department of Quantitative Analysis and Control split into two departments—Accounting and Management Information Systems and Applied Statistics and Operations Research. Departmental and curricular reorganization in the College of Education led to the forming of the new departments of Library and Education Media, Administration and Supervision, Curriculum and Instruction, and Foundations and Inquiry. One other important change was the elevation in 1975 of the forty year old Graduate School to the Graduate College—a clear reflection of the growing size and importance of graduate education.[43]

As a result of a number of forces operating—the enrollment cap, the 1976 Master Plan, the demands for technical education, the women's movement—the university increased its efforts at providing evening and extramural opportunities. As program offerings expanded the organizational structure changed and consolidated so that by near the end of the 1970s an Office of Continuing Education and Regional and Summer Programs had emerged which coordinated courses on television, extension courses, non-credit adult education, Summer transition, and evening credit programs among others. For a few years a special effort was made to help women who were post-college age and wished to enter the salaried work force. This was done through the creation of a Center for Continuing Education for Women which opened its doors on South Main Street in downtown Bowling Green. The university also cooperated in the development of technical education by supporting the development of technical colleges in Northwest Ohio and then phasing out its Academic Centers. By 1973 all three Centers—Bryan, Fostoria, and Fremont — had been closed and their responsibilities absorbed by technical colleges. In one case, Firelands, the decision was made to increase involvement including technical education. This resulted by the middle of the 70s in the creation of Firelands College composed of three departments, Natural and Social Sciences, Humanities, and Applied Sciences, as an integral part of Bowling Green. On a related but somewhat different tangent in 1978 a coordinated program of cooperative education was launched which appreciably increased the on-the-job training/intern opportunities for all students. One other program, the Senior Adult Grants for Education (SAGE), was launched in 1976. The program was entirely service oriented since it, on a non-credit, space available basis, opened any course free of charge to any person sixty years of age or older.[44]

Another dimension of the changes occurring internally was mirrored in the number and variety of degrees at both the graduate and undergraduate levels that evolved during the 1970s. As President Moore assumed the presidency the university offered a total of eighteen different degrees evenly divided between graduate and undergraduate levels. Of the graduate degrees seven were at the Masters' level, one was a Specialists, and the other the Doctor of Philosophy (Ph.D.). Five departments offered the Ph.D. - Biology, Educational Administration, English, Psychology, and Speech. At the time of Moore's death Bowling Green awarded forty two different degrees with twenty nine of them being undergraduate and thirteen being graduate. The substantial increase from eight to twenty five baccalaureate degrees was largely an outgrowth of the creation of the College of Health and Community Services with its wide array of specialized programs. By 1981 four more areas were offering the Ph.D., three of which were departmental—History, Mathematics and Statistics, and Sociology—and one was interdisciplinary— American Culture. In 1979 a $220,000 National Endowment for the Humanities Grant enabled the Department of Philosophy to initiate a unique master's level degree program in Applied Philosophy. A recognition of the growing academic merit of Bowling Green and its programs emerged clearly during the Moore administration. In 1975 the top national honorary in the sciences and mathematics, Sigma Xi, established a chapter on the campus and in 1980 the oldest national honorary in the nation, Phi Beta Kappa, indicated that it would consider the university for a chapter. The process involved almost three years before final approval was voted on in August, 1982.[45]

While the Moore administration could point to many accomplishments there were also failures and frustrations. A major disappointment to the administration was the inability owing to "fears and political concerns" to create a School or College of Communications or Mass Communications which would have included Journalism, Marketing, Popular Culture, and Speech. A decade later in a somewhat different form the idea reached fruition when the School of Mass Communication was formed. During the mid-1970s the Department of Home Economics became so discordant that Provost Rothe threatened to abolish the department and distribute its academic responsibilities to various other units. Temporarily the department was functionally divided while a task force investigated the situation. By 1978 a chastened department under new leadership was functioning as a unit again. Organizational and morale problems also afflicted the Firelands College as it sought its role within the framework of the university. One other frustration was the slowdown and then halt in the authorization by the Board of Regents of doctoral programs. Only one new doctorate was approved by the Regents, American Culture, after the early 1970s, even though at least ten departments contemplated programs and several even developed complete proposals.[46]

Beyond the Purely Academic
Services and People

Essential elements of any university beyond its academic programs are the atmosphere that exists, the services available to all, and the character of its people. During the 1970s President Moore attempted to maintain and further develop an exciting and stimulating campus environment through a number of different approaches. He continued the effort to make the student body more international in nature by attacting more foreign students and creating new opportunities for student exchanges. While the numbers involved did not increase appreciably there was a slow growth in movement both ways which was bolstered in the late 70s when an exchange program was worked out with the Ecole Superieure de Commerce et d'Administration des Enterprise in Nantes, France. Another move to improve the residential nature of the campus was made in the Spring of 1979 when the weekly class schedule grid was altered so as to eliminate largely the four-day class schedule. The president argued that the revision made sense since it better utilitized the physical plant, but also because it lessened the likelihood of large numbers of students leaving on Thursday, thus creating a "loss of style and flavor." Although there was a considerable negative student reaction to the idea it was implemented in the Fall of 1979. An earlier approach to influencing the flavor of the student body was the initiation in 1973 of an appreciably enhanced scholarship program. Prior to that date a limited program based strictly on need was in use with the individual awards being modest. The new program instituted a no-need approach aimed at attracting the most academically talented students possible by offering full fee grants. The program awarded thirty four scholarships the first year and over the next four years increased the number to 148. Late in the decade the university added a program which gave a supplemental grant to the Ohio Board of Regents Scholarship students who enrolled at Bowling Green. The net result of the scholarship program of the 1970s was to attract in excess of 200 top scholars who it was hoped would enhance the academic level of the student body. This increased emphasis on academic tone was reflected in one other way with a renewed stress on honor students. In 1977 an Honors' floor in Mac Donald North was designated and the following year a university honors program was reinstituted.[47]

Among the vital services provided for students and faculty is the library. By the beginning of the 1970s the University Library was functioning well in its new quarters, although some major adjustments were still to be made. During the decade the library was faced with the problems of the university - unreliable financial support and a stable faculty and student body. Even so it continued to expand its holdings, budget, and services at the rate of approximately five percent per year. This dichotomy of a growing library and a stable patronage was clearly seen in the statistics of the decade. The total collection increased from 1,429,675 to 2,352,426 items of all sorts while the budget grew from \$1,297,322 to \$2,352,426, and yet circulation only grew from 427,638 in 1970 to 436,743 in 1980 and the patron count decreased by a little over 150,000 for those years. The decade witnessed a significant growth for the university in special and specialized collections in the areas of popular culture, rare books, the Great Lakes, Northwest Ohio, state and federal documents, and recordings. This overall expansion and specialization might explain why total interlibrary loans increased sixty five percent during the 70s while total borrowing by Bowling Green decreased by seventeen percent. One important change occurred when the library ended the original division of its collections into lower and upper/graduate holdings and integrated them totally by subject areas.[48]

An efficient means of registering students and a helpful system of advising them has plagued large universities for years. Major efforts to improve both were made in the 70s although dissatisfaction remained as the 80s began. After considerable study the university moved to computer-assisted registration for the Fall of 1971; an approach which appreciably lessened the number of students who had to stand in line. The system was constantly updated so that service rendered, even though not perfect, was dramatically improved. Advising, too, was overhauled through the use of the University Division and the expansion of that function at the college level.[49]

While the Moore administration sincerely believed in the importance of the individual—student, faculty, and staff—it fell into the management approach of grouping all people at the university as human resources. Using that composite approach, what was its general composition during the period 1970 to 1981?

Enrollment during the decade of the 70s grew slowly from a little over 16,000 to 17,659 with the growth being almost equally divided between the freshman class and all other undergraduate and graduate levels. In 1970 the freshmen came from seventy six of the eighty eight counties of Ohio and from nineteen states. The figures for 1980 for all students show eighty six of the eighty eight counties represented, forty six states, and fifty five foreign countries. As had been true during the 60s the primary counties represented were Cuyahoga, Lucas, Wood, Montgomery, and Franklin. The rank order changed somewhat during the decade with Cuyahoga remaining clearly ahead but Wood moving in front of Lucas and Franklin past Montgomery. Among the states students from New York were most numerous while Pennsylvania, New Jersey, Michigan, and by 1980 Illinois jockeyed for the other top positions. The quality of the students entering the university during the 1970s is a little difficult to judge since the general level of pre-college testing scores declined during the decade nationally. The figures indicate that in 1970, of the entering freshmen, 72% scored at 21.0 or higher on the ACT Test, with a total composite score for all new freshmen being 22.6, which was 2.6 points above the national average. Of that class, 64.3% were from the upper 30th percentile of their high school class. The total figures for incoming freshmen fluctuated somewhat during the middle of the decade, but stood in 1980 with 50% above 21.0 on the ACT, with a composite score of 20.4 which was 1.7 above the national average. Although the ACT scores were down substantially, the percentage drop in terms of high school class standing had declined only to 60.7% in the upper 30th percentile. Another possible indication of the quality of the student body can be seen in the grade point averages for the period. Much controversy surrounds the statistics—were the students better or was grading easier? The cold figures were for university-wide GPAs: 1970 - 2.66; 1972 - 2.84; 1975 - 2.77; and 1980 - 2.70. Interestingly, the high point was in 1972-73 when the best freshman class statistically was in its junior year. A further meaningful attempt at quality was the initiation for the Fall of 1977 of the Graduate Record Examination as a requirement for admission to the Graduate College.

The undergraduate enrollment pattern changed radically in a number of ways during the 70s. In 1970 the College of Education maintained its historic leadership position with 6725 undergraduate students, followed by Arts and Sciences with 3505, Business with 2444, the School of Music with 292, and the Graduate School with 1708. In 1975 the comparable figures were Education 4738, A & S 3981, Business 3852, Music 434, the new College of Health and Community Services 874, and the now Graduate College 1999. By 1980 the enrollment had altered so that Business led with 4768, followed by A & S 4215, Education 3603, Health and Community Services 1354, Music 408, and Graduate 2100. Another major modification occurred when in January 1973 the university adopted a sex-blind admission policy. That policy and the increased number of women entering new fields led to a sex shift in enrollments from fifty-two/forty-eight percent men at the undergraduate level in 1970 to fifty-eight/forty-two women in 1980, and at the graduate level from thirty two point seven percent women to forty six percent in 1980. These movements were not only in numbers and percentages but in areas. While more women than men entered fields formerly assumed to be dominated by one sex, movement both ways occurred. Although the number was small, men began to enroll in both nursing and home economics while a much larger number of women entered the field of business.

The ultimate goal of the university is not in how many students it matriculates but in how many it graduates. When President Moore asumed office Bowling Green had awarded a total of 34,113 degrees, 29,365 of which were baccaluareate, 4559 masters, 109 specialist, and 80 doctoral. The Spring that he died, 1981, the comparable figures were 74,556 total with bachelors being 60,945, masters 12,601, specialists 280, and doctoral 730. Also during the decade of the 70s some 1200 associate degrees were awarded at the main campus and the Firelands College.[50]

The size of the faculty and staff during the 1970s remained stable at around 2150. During the decade the mix changed as the needs of the university shifted and economic pressures dictated. The result was an increase in the total number of faculty of forty two and of the contract (professional) staff of fifty three while the classified (civil service) staff declined by one hundred. Of the faculty approximately sixty percent were tenured in 1970 as opposed to sixty eight percent in 1980, while the percentage with doctoral degrees grew slightly from the upper sixties to the low seventies.[51]

As the decade of the 70s progressed tensions concerning the composition of the entire university staff, and especially the faculty, increased. The pressure centered on the number of women and minorities represented, and on the question of equitable treatment. In the Spring of 1971 several women faculty charged that discrimination existed at the university against women and was demonstrably evident in salaries, promotions, tenure, administrative positions, and even admission policy. Early in the Fall of 1971 the Faculty Senate formed an Ad Hoc Committee on the Status of Women which submitted a report to the Senate in May, 1972. The report held that there was "substantial evidence to suggest pattern discrimination by sex in hiring, promotion, tenure, rank, numbers, and salary."[52] The Faculty Senate supported the recommendations of the committee which called for positive action to rectify those abuses that did exist. While the administration was dealing with aspects of the report it was hit on November 2, 1972 with charges filed with the Department of Health, Education, and Welfare by the Women's Equity Action League (WEAL) alleging that women as a class were discriminated against in admissions, financial aid, student placement, hiring, tenure, promotion, and salary. Even though the Office of Civil Rights reported in 1978 "that it did not find that a preponderance of evidence indicated that women are discriminated against,"[53] a number of alterations did occur that assured greater fairness. Among the changes were: the appointment of a Director of Equal Opportunity, a special salary allowance for women to correct past inequities, the development of an Affirmative Action Program, the initiation of a sex-blind admission policy, and an increase in the percentage of women new hires to faculty and administrative/contract positions. In the last category, however, the actual number of women faculty employed in 1980 had risen only slightly from that of 1972. At the very end of the Moore administration one further step was taken with the official adoption in 1981 of a University Sexual Harassment Policy.[54]

While the employment and treatment of women was a distinct issue, it was a part of the larger concern of the rights of minorities. The 1970s witnessed a continual effort to increase minority employment. At the beginning of the decade an Office of Equal Opportunity was created which carried the main responsibility for developing and then administering an affirmative action program. The effort and support given to the recruiting of minority faculty and staff by the university was often a matter of dispute. The machinery to accomplish the task was in place and functioning, but the results were disappointing. After a substantial increase at the start of the 70s the number of new black faculty increased only slightly during the last half of the decade and stood in 1980 at thirty nine of whom twenty eight were male. A similar pattern existed among the contract and classified staff. Hispanic employment in all three categories was low although highest among the classified ranks.[55]

Despite the differences and turmoil over employment there were some positive developments that benefitted the faculty. In 1974 a faculty development program was initiated which was substantially enhanced when the state legislature in the Fall of 1976 authorized the use of state money to finance sabbatical leaves. This made possible the emergence of both faculty research and faculty improvement leave schemes that were begun by the 1977-78 academic year. The debate of the 60s between research and teaching resurfaced with these plans since the number of leaves were limited. Which would benefit the university most—money spent on research and probable publication or that invested in helping faculty become better teachers? As the 80s began a compromise had been reached in which some support was given to both. In the early 1980s two further changes evolved that held promise for the faculty. In 1980 a Faculty Development Center was established to serve as an agency that could help individuals with their professional and career development. The following year the university authorized the establishment of a Supplemental Retirement Program which allowed faculty to retire but continue to teach one quarter/semester a year for five more years or to age seventy. By the mid-1970s enrollment projections for the 1980s, which indicated a substantial decline in college bound high schoolers, triggered administrative moves to control staffing. The Provost proposed that professional competence alone was not sufficient grounds for granting tenure, but that the total needs of the university had to be considered as well. The Faculty Senate disagreed arguing that the size and collegiate distribution of the faculty should be managed through attrition and careful future planning and not by denying competent faculty, working in good faith, tenure because student demand in their disciplines had or might lessen. Following considerable consultation the Provost accepted the Faculty Senate position.[56]

Money, Money
More Is Not Always Enough

"Some say this one's the Year of the Crunch — others the Year of the Crash — I believe there's every chance it can be the Year of the Creative Response."[57]

While President Moore was talking about the 1971-1972 fiscal year he came eventually to realize that he was living in a decade that continually demanded creative financial responses. The university budget was constantly buffeted by inadequate state appropriations and a rising inflation rate while enrollment remained almost steady. Since state subsidies were enrollment driven the consequence of these forces was a continuing budget squeeze. The situation reached such critical proportions in four different fiscal years during the decade that special committees were formed to monitor budgetary practices. In late 1973 and early 1974 a major furor and temporary crisis erupted when the Board of Regents informed Bowling Green that $304,000 was going to be withheld from the subsidy payment because it was 450 students over its authorized FTE count. The issue was resolved by an Attorney General's opinion which held that such restrictions were not legally mandated by the legislature. One of the crisis years was 1976-77. In the Fall President Moore in an interview with an advanced journalism class commented that he had a "secret list" that he would use to trim the budget. When that report was printed there was a negative faculty reaction which led Moore in a memo to Provost Rothe to write:

"...it is true I responded much too fully and openly about the budget issue, and I have no excuse for that except that I have always agreed to meet with the advanced reporting classes for a session like this. So far, I have yet to enjoy the result!

He continued:

"Surely, if the blacks can forgive Jimmy Carter for "ethnic purity," the faculty can forgive its president who has introduced more openess in the budget process than any other president in the state of Ohio or in the history of this institution for that matter for misusing the word "secret" in a context where it could be so easily misunderstood."[58]

A cursory viewing of the figures would seem to belie fiscal problems in that the total university budget increased from almost $40 million in 1970-71 to $84 million in 1980-81 or by $44 million of which, however, only $18.5 million was from the state. The balance of the income for the total budget came from Instructional Fees which rose from $8 million in 1970-71 to $17.3 million in 1980-81, from substantially increased outside funding for research which for the same period went from $1.7 million to $5.1 million, and from general auxiliary accounts such as room and board which doubled from $17 million to $34 million in the 70s. Income from some other sources which were only a small portion of the total made life more pleasant and more productive. The annual Senior Challenge Campaign generated up to $50,000 a year while annual alumni giving soared from $89,000 in 1970 to $507,000 by 1980.[59]

Faculty salaries was an area of growth and controversy in the 70s. Average salaries for all ranks grew from $13,115 in 1970-71 to $27,792 in 1980-81 which was a forty seven percent increase, but was some four and a half percent less than the increase in the Consumer Price Index for the same period. During that same period the American Association of University Professors (AAUP) national salary ratings (one low/five high) found Bowling Green at the professorial level dropping from four to three, but at the instructor and assistant level rising from two to three. The loss of income to the CPI and the drop at the professorial level helped generate in 1976 and beyond a drive for collective bargaining for the faculty. In November, 1978 President Moore asked the Board of Trustees to authorize such an election early in 1979. On January 25 and 26 ninety percent of the eligible faculty voted and turned down collective bargaining by a vote of 320 to 311. In the mid-seventies the administration attempted for two years to reward selected faculty and staff through a Special Achievement Award Program that recognized outstanding research and service with an additional merit pay increase. The program proved to be both expensive and demoralizing for the majority and was terminated.[60]

Expenses in a number of other areas increased as well. Classified staff wages were increased several times and on a few occasions without additional state funding being forthcoming. The 1970s witnessed three major bond sales which increased the bonded indebtedness of the university by $17.7 million although with the payments made during the decade on earlier issues the actual total increase by 1980 was only $10 million. A major source of expense was the spiraling cost of utilities. Between 1970 and 1980 the annual bill for utilities grew by $2.3 million in spite of significant success in cutting consumption in every category—water/sewage, gas, electricity, and coal. This was accomplished through computer monitoring of heating, decreasing lighting, shortening the work week in the summer to four and a half days thus shutting off air conditioning for two and a half days, and raising the energy consciousness of the campus. All those efforts did save the university an estimated $1 million plus in avoided costs. A substantial and memorable expense was incurred as a result of the "Blizzard of 1978" which generated in labor costs and property damage some $500,000 in additional charges on the budget.[61]

The growing size of the budget and the development of the Academic Charter led to a greater involvement of faculty and students in the entire budgeting process. An overall Advisory Committee on the Educational Budget was established and later in the decade two other advisory committees on the general fee and on residences and dining hall budgets. At the start of the 70s at the request of the Board of Regents the entire budgeting process was revamped to a Planned Programming Budget System which meshed with the standardized scheme they had developed.

Another facet of the appreciating cost of education was the demand it placed on students and their parents. While the actual percentage paid into the educational budget by students declined slightly during the 70s, the cash outlay increased. A significant factor in bridging this rise was the increase in support from the university, the state, and the federal government in the form of fee waivers, scholarships, grants, employment, and loans. The following rounded figures demonstate this well: University (including athletics) 1970 - $220,000, 1980 - $1.5

million; State (Ohio Instructional Grants) 1970-$187,000, 1980-$800,000; Federal (grants and loans) 1970 - $1 million, 1980 - $7.5 million. In addition, by 1980 university and federally supported employment had reached $2.6 million annually while guaranteed loans amounted to $13 million.[62]

Notes

Chapter IV

1. *BOT Min.,* May 13, 1970; *CAC - Hollis A. Moore,* Box 100, Folder 6; *BGN,* Vol. 54, #102, May 13, 1970, p. 1 & #103, May 14, 1970, p. 1; Lipset, *New Nation,* pp. VI-XI.

2. *CAC-HAM,* Box 32, Folder 64. (4/30/71).

3. *BGN,* Vol. 55, #11, Sept. 19, 1970, p. 1.

4. *CAC-HAM,* Box 32, Folders 47, 69, 87, 120, & 138, Box 33, Folders 147, 153, 158, 172, 173, & 178, Box 47, Notebook 1/72 - 12/74 & 1/75 - 12/80; *BGN,* Vol. 65, #2, Sept. 26, 1979.

5. *CAC-HAM,* Box 100, Folder 6.

6. *Ibid.,* Box 32, Folder 120. (9/23/74).

7. *MS-376,* #8.

8. *BGN,* Vol. 57, #76, Feb. 22, 1974, p. 2.

9. *MS-376,* #8c; *BOT Min.,* Aug. 28, 1971, Aug. 31, 1972, Dec. 15, 1973, July 11, 1974, Jan. 9, 1975, Aug. 27, 1975, May 13, 1976, April 14, 1977, June 9, 1979, Aug. 9, 1979, Oct. 11, 1979; *BGN,* Vol. 55, #105, April 9, 1971, p. 3, Vol. 57, #89, April 2, 1974, pp. 1-2, Vol. 58, #16, Oct. 6, 1974, p. 1., Vol. 59, #88, March 3, 1976, p. 1, Vol. 60, #21, Oct. 26, 1976, p. 7, #40, Dec. 1, 1976, p. 1.

10. *CAC-HAM,* Box 79, Folder 6.

11. *Ibid.; BOT Min.,* April 5, 1973, March 16, 1974, July 11, 1974, Jan. 8, 1976, May 13, 1976, Feb. 10, 1977, Sept. 30, 1977; *BGN,* Vol. 56, #6, Sept. 26, 1971, p. 17, Vol. 57, #82, March 5, 1974, p. 3, Vol. 58, #3, July 19, 1974, p. 1.

12. *MS-376,* #8c; *BOT Min.,* May 9, 1974, Aug. 27, 1975, Feb. 12, 1976, May 13, 1976, April 14, 1977, May 12, 1977, Sept. 30, 1977, May 18, 1978, Oct. 11, 1979, Aug. 7, 1980; *BGN,* Vol. 56, #11, Sept. 30, 1971, p. 5, #12, Oct. 1, 1971, p. 1, Vol. 57, #112, May 10, 1974, p. 1, Vol. 61, #4, Sept. 23, 1977, p. 9, #106, May 19, 1978, p. 1.

13. *BOT Min.,* Jan. 6, 1972, Dec. 15, 1973, Oct. 3, 1974, April 10, 1975, Sept. 30, 1977, Aug. 25, 1978, Oct. 11, 1979, March 13, 1980; *BGN,* Vol. 54, #129, Aug. 13, 1970, p. 1, Vol. 56, #23, Oct. 21, 1971, p. 1, #130, July 27, 1972, p. 1., Vol. 57, #4, July 26, 1973, p. 1, #113, May 14, 1974, p. 1, Vol. 60, #14, Oct. 13, 1976, p. 1, #18, Oct. 20, 1976, p. 1, #38, Nov. 23, 1976, p. 1, #103, May 5, 1977, p. 1, Vol. 61, #61, Feb. 14, 1978, p. 3, #87, April 18, 1978, p. 1.

14. *MS-376,* #8c; *BOT Min.,* Aug. 28, 1971, Aug. 31, 1972; *BGN,* Vol. 56, #18, Oct. 11, 1972, p. 1, Vol. 57, #118, May 22, 1974, p. 1.

15. *BOT Min.,* March 10, 1971, April 5, 1973, April 8, 1976, Oct. 21, 1976, April 19, 1979, Aug. 9, 1979, Aug. 7, 1980, Nov. 13, 1980; *BGN,* Vol. 65, #2, Sept. 26, 1975, p. 6.

16. *BOT Min.,* Oct. 2, 1970, Oct. 17, 1970, Nov. 6, 1970, July 7, 1971, April 27, 1972, Jan. 8, 1973, June 9, 1973, Oct. 5, 1973, Feb. 14, 1974, March 16, 1974, Aug. 25, 1978; *BGN.,* Vol. 56, #6, Sept. 26, 1971, p. 17, Vol. 61, #48, Jan. 18, 1978, p. 1, Vol. 65, #26, Nov. 8, 1979, p. 3, Vol. 66, #20, Oct. 28, 1980, p. 5.

17. *BOT Min.,* March 10, 1970, Nov. 6, 1970, May 10, 1971, Feb. 24, 1972, May 15, 1975, Oct. 11, 1979, Jan. 10, 1980, Aug. 7, 1980.

Notes

Chapter IV (cont'd.)

18. *Ibid.,* Oct. 5, 1973, Aug. 27, 1975, Jan. 8, 1976, May 13, 1976, Sept. 30, 1977, Jan. 18, 1979, May 17, 1979, Oct. 11, 1979, Jan. 10, 1980, March 12, 1981, May 8, 1981.

19. *CAC-HAM,* Box 32, Folder 64.

20. *Ibid.,* Box 47, Notebook 1/73 - 12/74.

21. *Ibid.,* Box 47, Notebook 1/75 - 12/80.

22. *BOT Min.,* Jan. 8, 1971, March 10, 1971, May 10, 1971, May 20, 1971, Feb. 24, 1972, Jan. 18, 1973, March 1, 1973, March 16, 1974, Aug. 25, 1978, Oct. 5, 1978, March 8, 1979; *BGN,* Vol. 55, #65, Jan. 12, 1971, p. 5, #98, March 11, 1971, p. 1, #129, May 21, 1971, p. 1., Vol. 56, #130, July 27, 1972, p. 1, #132, Aug. 10, 1972, p. 3, #42, Jan. 4, 1973, p. 1, #81, March 2, 1973, p. 1., Vol. 61, #122, Oct. 10, 1978, p. 1, #130, Oct. 24, 1978, p. 1; *MS-376,* #17 (Interview with Richard A. Edwards).

23. *BOT Min.,* July 7, 1971, April 27, 1972, Oct. 15, 1973, Nov. 7, 1974, May 15, 1975, Sept. 9, 1976, April 19, 1979; *BGN,* Vol. 55, #94, March 4, 1971, p. 2, #111, April 21, 1971, p. 1, #131, May 27, 1971, p. 1., Vol. 56, #59, Jan. 25, 1972, p. 2, #17, Oct. 10, 1972, p. 3., #72, Feb. 20, 1973, p. 1., Vol. 57, #53, Jan. 15, 1974, p. 1, #122, May 29, 1974, p. 1, Vol. 58, #18, Oct. 9, 1974, p. 3; MS-376, #17.

24. *Bulletin* - 1978-1979, p. 5.

25. *CAC-HAM,* Box 32, Folder 64, p. 3.

26. *Ibid.,* Box 32, Folders 47, 64, Box 33, Folder 153, Box 47, Notebook 1/73-12/74; *BOT Min.,* March 6, 1970; *BGN,* Vol. 55, #42, Nov. 4, 1970, p. 3, #58, Dec. 1, 1970, p. 1, #60, Dec. 3, 1970, p. 1, #62, Jan. 6, 1971, p. 3, #88, Feb. 23, 1971, p. 1, Vol. 59, #89, April 1, 1976, p. 1, Vol. 60, #75, March 2, 1977, p. 1; *RFS Annual Reports,* 1976-77 Annual Report.

27. *BOT Min.,* July 10, 1970; *BGN,* Vol. 54, #124, July 9, 1970, p. 1, Vol. 55, #22, Oct. 7, 1970, p. 3, #23, Oct. 8, 1970, p. 6.

28. *BOT Min.,* Oct. 2, 1970; *CAC-HAM,* Box 32, Folder 64, 4/30/71, Folder 87, 9/25/72; *CAC-MAP,* Box 1, Folder 1, Box 3, Folder 5; *MS-376,* 13d; *BGN,* Vol. 55, #13, Sept. 24, 1970, p. 6, #25, Oct. 13, 1970, p. 3, #36, Oct. 27, 1970, p. 1, #38, Oct. 29, 1970, p. 2, #39, Oct. 30, 1970, p. 1, #66, Jan. 13, 1971, p. 1, #67, Jan. 14, 1971, p. 1, #97, March 10, 1971, p. 1, #118, May 4, 1971, p. 3, #133, May 28, 1971, p. 3, Vol. 56, #6, Sept. 26, 1971, p. 1, #13, Oct. 5, 1971, p. 1, #29, Nov. 2, 1971, p. 1, #31, Nov. 4, 1971, p. 1, #32, Nov. 5, 1971, p. 3, #52, Jan. 12, 1972, p. 1, #67, Feb. 8, 1972, p. 3, #126, June 29, 1972, p. 1, #115, May 17, 1973, p. 3, Vol. 57, #15, Oct. 5, 1973, p. 4.

29. *CAC-MAP,* Box 3, Folder 5. "The Redefined Baccalaureate: A Proposal for the Establishment of a Modular Achievement Program at Bowling Green State University." p. 12.

30. *CAC-CUE,* Box 1, Folder 2. "The First Year of the CUE Center: A Synopsis" 9/11/75.

31. *BOT Min.,* Oct. 24, 1972, Jan. 18, 1973, March 1, 1973, Oct. 5, 1973, July 11, 1974, Oct. 3, 1974, Jan. 9, 1975, May 15, 1975, Aug. 27, 1975; *MS-376,* 13e and 43; *BGN.* Vol. 54, #125, July 16, 1970, p. 1, Vol. 55, #96,

Notes

Chapter IV (cont'd.)
March 9, 1971, p. 1, Vol. 56, #52, Jan. 12, 1972, p. 1, #15, Oct. 5, 1972, p. 1, #19, Oct. 12, 1972, p. 5, #43, Nov. 30, 1972, p. 1, #66, Feb. 6, 1973, p. 1., #67, Feb. 7, 1973, pp. 1 & 4, Vol. 57, #40, Nov. 20, 1973, p. 1, Vol. 58, #27, Oct. 24, 1974, p. 1, #50, Jan. 10, 1975, p. 1, #104, April 17, 1975, p. 1.

32. *BOT Min.*, Oct. 11, 1979; *Fac Sen. Coll,* Box 10, Nov. 2, 1971, Dec. 7, 1971 (Attch.), Jan. 4, 1972, May 1972, Box 11, Dec. 4, 1979, Jan. 15, 1980, Feb. 5, 1980, March 4, 1980, April 15, 1980 (Attch.), April 29, 1980, June 3, 1980; *CAC - Councils and Committees, (Academic Council Minutes)* Box 7, Nov. 29, 1972 (Attch.), Box 8, Nov. 20, 1974, Dec. 4, 1974, Oct. 22, 1975 (Attch.), Oct. 29, 1975 (Attch.), Box 25, April 2, 1980, April 16, 1980 (Attch), April 30, 1980, May 7, 1980 (Attch.), May 21, 1980, May 28, 1980, June 4, 1980 (Attch.), June 12, 1980, July 23, 1980; *BGN,* Vol. 56, #11, Sept. 30, 1971, p. 2, #41, Nov. 23, 1971, p. 3, #63, Nov. 30, 1972, p. 1, #46, Dec. 7, 1972, p. 1, Vol. 58, #43, Nov. 21, 1974, p. 1, #46, Dec. 5, 1974, p. 1, Vol. 65, #2, Sept. 26, 1979, p. 1, #21, Oct. 31, 1979, p. 1, #81, April 4, 1980, p. 1, #95, April 30, 1980, p. 1, #100, May 8, 1980, p. 1, #103, May 14, 1980, p. 1.

33. *CAC-MAP,* "Report of The Committee on Introductory Studies, Bowling Green State University." Spring, 1972, p. 5.

34. *MS-376,* Number 44.

35. *Ibid.,* Number 29.

36. *Ibid.,* Numbers 29 and 44; *CAC-MAP,* Box 3, Folder 5; *BOT Min.,* Aug. 7, 1980; *BGN,* Vol. 56, #115, May 17, 1973, p. 3, #125, June 21, 1973, p. 1, Vol. 57, #24, Oct. 23, 1973, p. 1, #34, Nov. 8, 1973, p. 2, #70, Feb. 13, 1974, p. 2.

37. *CAC-HAM,* Box 32, Folder 2.

38. *Ibid.,* Box 33, Folder 147.

39. *Ibid.,* Box 32, Folder 2; *CAC-ACM,* Box 8, Folder June-August, 1977 (8/17) and September, 1978-March, 1979 (11/1/78); *BOT Min.,* Aug. 7, 1980; *BGN,* Vol. 57, #102, April 24, 1974, p. 3, #115, May 16, 1974, p. 1, Vol. 61, #9, Oct. 4, 1977, p. 5, #36, Nov. 2, 1978, p. 1, #219, Jan. 18, 1979, p. 1, Vol. 65, #56, Feb. 5, 1980, p. 1, Vol. 66, #84, April 10, 1981, p. 1.

40. *CAC - Vice Provost for Student Affairs,* Box 34, Folder 19; *CAC-CC,* Box 8, Folder June-Aug. 1977; *BGN,* Vol. 55, #18, Oct. 1, 1970, p. 1, Vol. 56, #6, Sept. 26, 1971, p. 10, #13, Oct. 5, 1971, p. 1, #14, Oct. 6, 1971, p. 2, #20, Oct. 15, 1971, p. 1, #32, Nov. 5, 1971, p. 1, #63, Jan. 31, 1973, p. 1, #125, June 21, 1973, p. 1, Vol. 57, #58, Jan. 23, 1974, p. 1, Vol. 58, #36, Nov. 8, 1974, p. 1, Vol. 61, #22, Oct. 26, 1977, p. 1, Vol. 65, #26, Nov. 8, 1979, p. 1.

41. *CAC-HAM.* Box 47, Notebook 1/73-12/74. "Community Speech." 4/26/73.

42. *Ibid.,* Box 32, Folder 2. "Provost's Report on the Years 1973-77."

43. *Ibid; BOT Min.* July 10, 1970, Feb. 5, 1971, May 20, 1971, July 7, 1971, Oct. 14, 1971, Nov. 18, 1971, April 5, 1973, May 3, 1973, Jan. 9, 1975, May 15, 1975, May 18, 1978, Aug. 25, 1978, March 8, 1979, Aug. 9, 1979, Aug. 7, 1980; *BGN.* Vol. 55, #14, Sept. 25, 1970, p. 4, Vol. 58, #114, May 1, 1975, p. 6, Vol. 61, #106, May 19, 1978, p. 1, #248, March 9, 1979, p. 1.

Notes

Chapter IV (cont'd.)
44. *BOT Min.,* Feb. 5, 1971, March 1, 1973, May 13, 1976, July 8, 1976, Oct. 2, 1980; *BGN,* Vol. 57, #125, June 20, 1974, p. 1, Vol. 65, #7, Oct. 4, 1979, p. 3.
45. *MS-376,* #13; CAC-Phi Beta Kappa, Boxes 1 & 2; *BOT Min.,* Feb. 5, 1971, May 20, 1971, July 7, 1971, Feb. 24, 1972, March 18, 1972, April 27, 1972, Aug. 16, 1973, Dec. 15, 1973, Jan. 9, 1975, May 15, 1975, Aug. 27, 1975, May 13, 1976, July 28, 1977, Aug. 9, 1979, Jan. 10, 1980, March 13, 1980; *BGN,* Vol. 55, #81, Feb. 9, 1971, p. 1, Vol. 56, #20, Oct. 15, 1971, p. 1, Vol. 59, #78, Feb. 27, 1976, p. 1.
46. *CAC-HAM,* Box 32, Folder 2, p. 4 & passim; *BOT Min.,* March 13, 1975, April 14, 1977, July 28, 1977; *BGN,* Vol. 56, #81, March 2, 1973, p. 1, #110, May 9, 1973, p. 1, Vol. 57, #54, Jan. 16, 1974, p. 1, #55, Jan. 17, 1974, p. 1, #104, April 26, 1974, p. 1, #110, May 8, 1974, p. 1, #120, May 24, 1974, p. 2, Vol. 58, #17, Oct. 8, 1974, p. 3, #18, Oct. 9, 1974, p. 2, #56, Jan. 22, 1975, p. 1, Vol. 59, #109, May 6, 1976, p. 1, Vol. 60, #100, April 29, 1977, p. 1, #115, May 26, 1977, p. 1.
47. *MS-376,* #7; *CAC-HAM,* Box 32, Folder 138, Speech, Sept. 20, 1976; *BOT Min.,* March 2, 1978; *BGN,* Vol. 56, #23, Oct. 21, 1971, p. 1, #38, Nov. 17, 1971, p. 1, Vol. 58, #114, May 1, 1975, p. 6, Vol. 64, #279, May 22, 1979, p. 2, Vol. 57, #58, Jan. 23, 1974, p. 1, Vol. 59, #120, July 8, 1976, p. 1, Vol. 60, #96, April 22, 1977, p. 1, Vol. 61, #118, Sept. 22, 1978, p. 1; *CAC-HAM,* Box 47, Notebook 1/73-12/74, Remarks to Fac. Sen.; *BOT Min.,* May 15, 1975, Jan. 5, 1978.
48. *MS-376,* 11, 11a, 11b, 11c, 11d, & 11e.
49. *CAC-HAM,* Box 33, Folder 173, 9/24/79; *BGN,* Vol. 55, #51, Nov. 17, 1970, p. 1, Vol. 56, #48, Jan. 4, 1973, p. 1.
50. *MS-376,* 10, 10a, 10c-f; *CAC-HAM,* Box 47, Notebook 1/73-12/74, 1/9/73; *Research Services Annual Report, 1976-77; BGN,* Vol. 56, #6, Sept. 26, 1971, p. 16, #51, Jan. 10, 1973, p. 1, #55, Jan. 17, 1973, p. 3, Vol. 61, #228, Feb. 2, 1979, p. 1.
51. *MS-376,* #9 & 9b.
52. *BGN,* Vol. 56, #123, p. 1. See also *Fac Sen Coll,* Box 10. Fac Sen Min., Dec. 7, 1971 & attachment.
53. *BOT Min.,* May 18, 1978.
54. *Ibid.,* April 27, 1972; *Fac Sen Coll.,* Box 10, Fac Sen Min., Dec. 7, 1971 & May 30, 1972; *BGN,* Vol. 55, #99, March 12, 1971, p. 1, #103, April 6, 1971, p. 1, Vol. 56, #23, Oct. 21, 1971, p. 1, #50, Jan. 7, 1972, p. 5, #115, May 17, 1972, p. 1, #123, May 31, 1972, p. 1, Vol. 56, #14, Oct. 4, 1972, p. 1, #22, Oct. 18, 1972, p. 1, #43, Nov. 30, 1972, p. 1, #44, Dec. 5, 1972, p. 1, #45, Dec. 6, 1972, p. 1, #75, Feb. 21, 1973, pp. 1 & 3, #89, April 3, 1973, p. 1, Vol. 61, #6, Sept. 28, 1977, p. 1, Vol. 61, #45, Jan. 15, 1981, p. 1, Vol. 62, #120, Oct. 13, 1981, p. 5.
55. *BGN,* Vol. 56, #30, Oct. 31, 1972, p. 1, Vol. 60, #62, Feb. 8, 1977, p. 1, #86, April 6, 1977, p. 1, #92, April 15, 1977, p. 1, Vol. 66, #7, Oct. 3, 1980, p. 1, #18, Oct. 23, 1980, pp. 1 & 3.
56. *CAC-HAM,* Box 32, Folder 2, Provost Report, 1973-74; *Fac Sen Coll.,* Box 10. Minutes of Jan. 8 & 22, March 5, 1974; *BOT Min.,* Nov. 7, 1974,

Notes

Chapter IV (cont'd.)
April 14, 1973, Nov. 9, 1979, Aug. 7, 1980, Jan. 8, 1981; *BGN,* Vol. 57, #5, Jan. 11, 1974, pp. 1 & 3, #84, March 7, 1974, p. 1, #107, May 2, 1974, p. 1, Vol. 60, #5, Sept. 28, 1976, p. 1, Vol. 61, #22, Oct. 26, 1977, p. 1, #237, Feb. 20, 1979, p. 1, Vol. 65, #50, Jan. 24, 1980, p. 1, Vol. 61, #42, Jan. 9, 1981, p. 1.

57. *CAC-HAM,* Box 32, Folder 69. Address entitled "State of the University."

58. *Ibid.,* Box 32, Folder 1. Also, *CAC-HAM,* Box 47, Notebook 1/73-12/74, March 1974, Notebook 1/75-12/80, May 9, 1975 memo; *BOT Min.,* Oct. 14, 1971, Jan. 6, 1972, Nov. 6, 1975, May 12, 1977, Jan. 10, 1980, Nov. 13, 1980, Jan. 8, 1981, & March 12, 1981; *BGN,* Vol. 55, #130, May 26, 1971, p. 1, Vol. 56, #6, Sept. 26, 1971, p. 3, #52, Jan. 12, 1972, p. 1, #71, Feb. 14, 1972, p. 1, #73, Feb. 19, 1972, p. 1, #77, Feb. 24, 1972, p. 1, Vol. 59, #27, Nov. 7, 1975, p. 1, Vol. 60, #2, Sept. 22, 1976, p. 1, #26, Nov. 3, 1976, p. 1, #33, Nov. 10, 1976, p. 1, Vol. 61, #86, April 14, 1978, p. 1, Vol. 65, #7, Oct. 4, 1979, p. 1, #126, Aug. 28, 1980, p. 1, Vol. 66, #28, Nov. 11, 1980, p. 1, #31, Nov. 14, 1980, p. 1, #39, Dec. 4, 1980, pp. 1 & 2, #43, Jan. 8, 1981, p. 1.

59. *MS-376,* Numbers 5, 6, 6a, and 6d.

60. *Ibid.,* #9a; CAC-HAM, Box 32, Folder 2, Provost Report, 1973-7; *BOT Min.,* Oct. 5, 1978, March 8, 1979; *Fac Sen Coll.,* Box 11, Minutes, Nov. 7, 1978, Jan. 16, 1979, Jan. 23, 1979 & Feb. 6, 1979; *BGN,* Vol. 61, #59, Feb. 9, 1978, p. 1, #88, March 19, 1978, p. 1, #122, Oct. 5, 1978, p. 1, #136, Nov. 2, 1978, p. 1, #141, Nov. 10, 1978, p. 1, #225, Jan. 30, 1979, p. 1; *CAC-HAM,* Box 47, Notebook, 1/75-12/80, Statement by HAM.

61. *MS-376,* #2; *CAC-HAM,* Box 47, Notebook 1/75-12/80, May 5, 1975, Memo; *BOT Min.,* Jan. 9, 1975, May 15, 1975, Oct. 21, 1976, Jan. 5, 1978, March 2, 1978, April 24, 1980; *BGN,* Vol. 57, #39, Nov. 16, 1973, p. 1, Vol. 59, #9, Feb. 27, 1976, p. 1, Vol. 60, #56, Jan. 27, 1977, p. 1, #57, Jan. 28, 1977, p. 1, #69, Feb. 18, 1977, p. 1, Vol. 61, #56, Feb. 3, 1978, p. 1, #61, Feb. 14, 1978, p. 1, #62, Feb. 15, 1978, p. 1, #65, Feb. 21, 1978, p. 3, #72, March 3, 1978, p. 1.

62. *BOT Min.,* Oct. 2, 1970, Feb. 5, 1971, May 3, 1973, Jan. 1, 1974; *MS-376,* #7.

CHAPTER V

"...WORTHY SONS AND DAUGHTERS"
The Student Scene During the 1970s

Student Protests — The Early 1970s

128

CHAPTER V

"...WORTHY SONS AND DAUGHTERS"
The Student Scene During the 1970s

The decade of the Moore administration seemed at its conclusion to have been a much calmer period than that of President Jerome. In retrospect, however, it was just as interspersed with controversy and strain, the chief difference being that the number of students involved tended to decline. While there was recurring tension through the whole period there were many positive moments, as well, ranging from Dave Wottle's gold medal in 1972 to the awarding of a chapter of Phi Beta Kappa in the early 1980s.

Woes or a Raised Consciousness?

"This could be an exciting year and we must move with a sense of urgency instead of panic."[1]

As President Moore in the Fall of 1970 faced his first full year on campus a state of relative, if anxious, calm seemed to prevail. The durability of the calm was uncertain and challenges to its continuance arose immediately. In early October William Kunstler addressed a large crowd in Anderson Arena in which he charged President Nixon and others of attempting to suppress honest dissent. He added that even the university had attempted to cancel his appearance; a charge denied by James Bond. A month later another large gathering in Anderson listened to Jane Fonda praise the Black Panthers and call for a peaceful revolution. During that same period four different bomb threats were made on campus by individuals claiming to be Weathermen or opposed to government recruiting of students. By Thanksgiving these activities stopped and all remained relatively quiet until April of 1971.[2]

129

As the first anniversary of the shootings at Kent State neared anti-war activity on campus renewed. In late April President Moore was handed a list of five demands drawn up by a group calling itself the "Concerned People of BGSU." It called for the president to issue a statement opposing continued involvement in Vietnam and a proposed state legislative bill on campus disturbances. Additionally, a ban on military recruiting on campus and the continued carrying of arms by the university police was demanded. Moore responded negatively to the group's appeal while also supporting the initiation of an information clarification system named Fact Line.

The April 30th issue of the *BG News* editorially called for a peaceful strike on May 4 and 5 to commemorate the Kent State shooting. On the evening of the 4th an estimated 2000 students gathered on campus and then marched to the four corners downtown where they remained for awhile before being persuaded by Mayor Gus Skibbie to move. The next stop was the area in front of the Court House where they remained for approximately three hours with riot police standing in the background before finally returning to the campus. The following evening a smaller crowd of around 600 held a rally on the steps of Williams Hall. Following it a group of the demonstrators marched to Memorial Hall where they broke into the building, but later left. Upon leaving about sixty of the number camped out in front of the building and pledged to remain there until after the upcoming ROTC Review on May 18th. They further called for the removal of ROTC from the campus and for the ending of credit for ROTC courses; a position which the *News* immediately supported editorially. On the 18th the review was held in the area behind Memorial Hall with parts of the field having been roped off for spectators. Near the end of the ceremony a large number of spectators spilled out on the field which caused President Moore to terminate the activity. The demonstrators in front of Memorial Hall following the review decided to continue their vigil until action was taken on the presence of ROTC and on credit. The same night, the 18th, they were briefly visited by William Kunstler who told them "What you do here..one tiny demonstration..is as significant as anything else in the world."[3] During the last ten days of May the events of earlier in the month tended to reach a climax. President Moore condemned the disruption of the review, the Academic Council referred the issue of ROTC credit to the Curriculum Committee of the College of Business, the demonstrators ended their vigil, and the university issued arrest warrants to twenty-one individuals, nineteen of whom were students, for their part in the ROTC melee.[4]

The 1971-72 school year was only slightly less fraught with tension than the preceding two years. A tone of discontent was set in the Fall when one of the Chicago Seven, John Froines, in an address called for the "eviction of Nixon." A further example appeared with an attack on the relatively new Senior Challenge Program by the *BG News*. Editorially *The News* asserted that "It is hard to believe that this organization is run by students who obviously have so much apple-pie love for this university that they feel it is their duty to dip in the pockets of their peers."[5] Mixed emotions buffeted the campus in December when hearings over the May ROTC arrests culminated in nineteen of the twenty-one either pleading guilty or no contest. Some faculty raised questions about selective arrests and the use of the Student Code to intimidate students. The turmoil continued in January, 1972 when the College of Business endorsed its Curriculum Committee's recommendation to continue granting academic credit to ROTC courses. *The News* commented sarcastically "We would like to commend the College of Business Curriculum Committee for completely living up to our expectations."[6] As May 4 approached calls for the president to condemn militarism, racism, and sexism resurfaced as did those for a boycotting of classes on the 4th. The Kent State commemoration attracted 2000 individuals to Anderson Arena to hear Rennie Davis attack the Nixon Administration. The meeting was followed again by a procession of an estimated 600 from the campus to downtown and back to the Sterling Farm where a symbolic bomb crater was dug. A final flareup occured on May 9th and 10th when groups of students first occupied the tenth floor of the Administration Building and then Memorial Hall. Simultaneously, a bomb threat was made and three fires were set on campus. Partially in response to these actions President Moore sent a telegram to President

Nixon stating that a continuation of the war posed a threat to the functioning of universities. Just as the academic year neared its end demands arose from a new source—black athletes, who called for greater financial aid, more representation in the athletic area, and increased help in the academic support areas. Most of these issues were resolved by the time school resumed in the fall.[7]

From the Spring of 1973 through the rest of the Moore administration there was continual contention concerning the rights and treatment of minorities and the role of the university police. By the Spring of 1973 it had become clear that there was considerable disarray in the minority student program area. It encompassed a wide range running from pre-college preparation to recruitment to academic advisement and much more. Additionally, it had developed rapidly and in a somewhat disjointed manner with the consequence that there was little centrality of direction or philosophy. During the Summer and Fall of 1973 the new Provost, Kenneth Rothe, grappled with the situation which after considerable controversy and some recrimination led to several resignations and the appointment in early 1974 of Charles L. Means as Vice Provost for Minority Affairs. He was charged with administering all minority programs.[8]

From early in 1975 until the end of 1977 the university police were the focus of several disputes. The earliest controversy was the perennial one of the necessity of weapons in a university community. The growing incidence of crime committed by non-students largely deflected that issue. Subsequent upon the continued carrying of arms by the police arose a question about the type of ammunition that should be used which generated much debate and study, but did not result in any change except for the creation of a University Police-Community Advisory Commitee which did continue to serve in a liaison capacity. Early in 1977 the Black Student Union charged that the university police were both over zealous and insensitive in their contact with black students. The initial complaint did not elicit an immediate response, but by April tensions had mounted to the point that the Board of Trustees agreed to investigate the various allegations. While BSU leaders objected to the make-up of the investigating committee they generally cooperated with its work.

A report was submitted to the Board in November which asserted that the problems between the police and the university community were serious to grave. The report recommended a number of changes including: renaming the police organization to the Department of Public Safety; increasing the use of sensitivity training for all police personnel; involving more students in its operations; and creating a board to review all police policies on an ongoing basis. The report also recognized that a number of past practices had been both questionable and insensitive. The major thrust of the entire report was that the university police had to place its primary emphasis on service and not on law enforcement. By the Spring of 1978 a new Director of Safety and Security was appointed and a major turnover of personnel had occurred.[9]

Contentiousness in relations between minorities and the university and among the various minority groups typified much of the period from the Spring of 1979 to that of 1981. On May 24, 1979 representatives of the Black Student Union, La Union De Estudiantes Latinos, the Third World Graduate Association, the African Peoples Association, and others presented twelve "demands" to the administration. The "demands" dealt with what was held to be "the consistent denial of our student rights." The charges ranged from concerns about racial discrimination in the graduate program to a call for race relation workshops and departmental status for the Ethnic Studies program. While tensions remained acute during May, discussions laid the ground for the resolution of a number of the concerns raised. During the following academic year, 1979-80, a Human Rights Commission was formed, several race relations workshops were held, a study of discrimination in graduate education was completed, Ethnic Studies attained departmental status, and arrangements with the city were made by which the university was to be notified when a minority student was arrested. Seemingly, the primary differences between the university and minority groups had been largely ameliorated when suddenly on April 28, 1980 President Moore was handed a twenty-one page set of "demands" by a group calling itself "The Committee on Latino Concerns."[10]

The complaints settled largely around the belief by Latino students that they were not being equitably treated either as a minority or in relation to the treatment afforded Blacks. The situation unexpectedly erupted when a group of Latinos occupied the President's office and the hallways of McFall Center and refused to leave. Twenty two of them were charged with trespass which was later dropped after they agreed to pay court costs. During the Summer of 1980 a committee investigated the full range of questions raised by the "demands." The chief recommendation, to consolidate the minority area operations within the various appropriate academic, financial, and student university offices, elicited strong opposition from the minority groups who posted such signs as–No SDP, No BGSU and SDP is Important, and led Provost Michael Ferrari to reject it. The report also called for a revamped Human Rights Commission which eventuated in another conflict between the president and the Latino Student Union over who should name the Latino representative. The issue was still unresolved at the time of Hollis Moore's death.[11]

At times, tensions over Vietnam, the place of ROTC on the campus, and the role and treatment of minorities seemed to dominate the campus scene. The Moore years were troubled by them, but maybe the university grew some in understanding and tolerance as a result. While the 1970s were tempered by those concerns Bowling Green also experienced much else of a more traditionally collegiate nature.

The Campus in the 1970s
Life Beyond Stress

"Through it all remember that the core of the learning process is not only cerebral and intellectual but also has to do with the opening of a personality to its full potentials and the making of a life style."[12]

The life style of students during the first half of the 70s as seen in the continuation of protest had much of the residual rebelliousness of the latter 60s about it. Then gradually a more conservative motif emerged. One of the more subtle but clear indications of this transformation occurred with the publication of Volume 60, Number 1 of *The BG News* on September 19, 1976 when for the first time since 1969 the words "An Independent Student Voice" did not appear on the masthead. The decade of the 1970s on campus was one of a mixture of attitudes, behavior, and experiences.

Some of the long standing campus traditions were bent, ignored, and satirized. Ironically or insightfully the theme for the 1970 Homecoming was "My, How We've Changed." The event was celebrated without the traditional floats, flags, or parades, and was only a foretaste of the 1974 event when a male student was elected Homecoming Queen much to the delight of some and the horror of others. A further reflection of the early 70s was seen in another *BG News* headline—"Greek system: fading, faltering but still here." Greeks and their role on campus did decline, but it proved to be only a phase for by 1980 the thirty one fraternities and sororities of 1970 had increased to forty. While some old traditions died or limped along in 1978 a new tradition was born when at the August commencement President Moore said: "Our June Commencement speaker, Erma Bombeck, began what I hope will be a tradition at B.G.S.U., I would like to ask the families of the graduates to rise so that we may all join in paying tribute to you."[13]

The changing life styles of college youth, or at least of some of their number, were greeted by the university with varying degrees of acceptance. A major concern especially of the first half of the 70s was drug usage — centered primarily on marijuana. The Board studied the problem in late 1971 in some depth, and in early 1972 a city-university group called the Committee on Drug Problems, Inc. established a Drug Problem Clinic near campus at 525 Pike Street which evolved in time into a general crisis prevention center called The Link. The use of drugs impacted significantly another campus activity - rock concerts. The student affairs area and student government wrestled constantly with the issue of drug usage and often subsequent rowdyism at concerts. The primary solution attempted was the use of student marshalls which had worked so well in the Spring of 1970. In general, however, the approach failed, and with that grew a reluctance on the part of the university to permit such concerts. While most of the concerts were small (2000 to 4000) and made up of primarily university audiences there was one major exception; The Poe Ditch Music Festival of 1975. The event was conceived of as a source of income for Intercollegiate Athletics through the rental of the stadium and as an end of the year celebration for the students. The concert, promoted by an outside group and widely advertised throughout the Midwest, attracted some 35,000, only ten percent of whom were Bowling Green students. The outcome was summarized well in the June 3rd *BG News* with the headline "Poe Ditch Music Festival -drugs, rain" and with the statement by President Moore that "The large scale rock concert experiment will not be repeated at Bowling Green State University. It was strictly a first time/last time experience."[14] The event had resulted in considerable damage to university property including the burning down of the press box at the Whittaker Track, and the influx of so many outsiders strained university/community relations.[15]

Another continuing problem from the late 60s that confronted the university was the demand for gynecological and birth control services. The opening of the Student Health Center with its many facilities made this request seem reasonable to many students. The university viewed the issue as two separate ones both of which had difficulties. However, in February 1973 a part time gynecologist from the Medical College of Ohio began seeing patients although the Health Center still did not stock contraceptives. By the later part of the decade the matter ceased being an issue for the student body.

The operation of the Health Center itself proved to be a center of concern during much of the 70s. When the center opened it was conceived of as an in-patient facility with 102 beds, six full time physicians, fourteen registered nurses, a pharmacy, and physical therapy program. However, the usage figures reported for the 1970-71 academic year showed that there had been 275 in-patients and 40,783 out-patients. Those figures proved to be an early indication that fixed costs were in excess of need. Considerable adjusting occurred over the next several years so that by 1977 the Health Center had become a predominantly out-patient facility whose services, in spite of the usual grumbling, were generally well rated by the student body. In 1980 a further service was added when the first collegiate "Wellness Center" in Ohio was opened.[16]

The 1970s were replete with many things that those who experienced them will long remember and in some cases, cherish.
These remembrances of things past ranged from major to
minor, but each was a part of the Bowling Green experience.
The most monumental of these by far was the "Blizzard of
1978." The storm which started early on Thursday morning,
January 26th as a rain and thunder storm escalated quickly into
a major blizzard which paralyzed much of Northwest Ohio,
knocking out electricity and many other vital services. Classes
were cancelled; staff was unable to reach campus; students were
isolated in their dorms; resourcefulness was called for. With
water off for some period of time sanitation became a problem
as did food preparation. Students pitched in to help cook, to
clean, and to shovel. Each individual has memories of the five
days of relative isolation, and many came in time to be a proud
owner of a "I Survived the Blizzard of '78" tee shirt.[17]
   The decade had its share of seemingly new, but often, in fact,
perennial collegiate occurrences and experiences. Among these
repetitions were the formation and demise yet again of another
veterans' organization, co-op bookstore, and shuttle bus
system. Similarly, the student frequented bars followed a
similar pattern. With the exception of Howard's Club H, by
the end of the 1970s all of the bars of the 60s had either
disappeared or changed names. The establishments most
patronized were J. Alfred's, the SOP, the Brathaus, the Uptown
and Downtown, the Longbranch, Sam B's, and up the road the
Dixie Electric Company. The entertainment varied during the
decade ranging from disco to country and western and from
female mud wrestling to male stripping. A continuing
concomitant of student drinking was rowdy behavior and
vandalism which in the 70s, as in earlier decades, led to
community complaints and threats of action.[18]
   A few other memorable facets of the period included the
university's creation in 1971 of the First Year of the Franchise
Committee which helped prepare students under twenty one for
their first opportunity to vote in a presidential election. The
mid-decade pressures of the women's movement and affirmative action led both Mortar Board and ODK to adopt sex-
blind membership criteria. Similarly, the Family Educational

Rights and Privacy Act of 1974 forced a policy of opening personal records to students while simultaneously making them less accessible to others. Of a quite different sort was the establishment in 1978 of On Campus Mail Boxes for all off campus students, which proved to be both personally convenient for the students and financially advantageous for the university. One last memorable event was the shock in April 1980 of the Exam Scam which involved an instructor and several fraternity students. The crisis was handled directly and openly by the university as a criminal act which elicited, generally, a favorable public reaction.[19]

Forward Falcons

A major part of the life of most university campuses is its involvement in athletics. President Moore shortly after assuming office stated "I strongly endorse the continuation of our broadly based athletic program..."[20] After an abortive start under the direction of a new Athletic Director the program continued to expand so that by 1980 the twelve intercollegiate sports of 1970 had burgeoned to twenty-four.

The year 1976 was in many ways a watershed year for university athletics. In that year women's teams that had been competing for several years entered full fledged intercollegiate competition, and were supported by a substantially increased budget. As a part of the increased sports' opportunities the intercollegiate athletic program was reorganized for financial and administrative reasons into two parts—the three revenue sports of basketball, football, and hockey and the other twenty one non-revenue sports. The year also saw a change in the leadership of two of the three revenue sports when Patrick Haley and Don Nehlen resigned from their head coaching positions of basketball and football and were replaced by John Weinert and Dennis Stolz respectively who were to guide teams for the next decade.[21]

During the decade Bowling Green teams had both great highs and frustrating lows, but consistently maintained an overall strong position in the Mid American Conference and elsewhere. The highs were too few, but oh how high they were. In the early

1970s track was supreme with both Sid Sink and Dave Wottle leading the way. Sink and Wottle set American and NCAA records in the 800 meters, the mile, the two mile, and the steeplechase, and in 1972 led Bowling Green to a second place finish in the NCAA Indoor Meet. The following September Wottle in a thrilling finish won the Gold Medal in the 800 meter run at the Munich Olympics. The same year in the spring Bowling Green garnered its only MAC All Sports Trophy (the Reese Cup) of the 1970s when the golf team, the tennis team, and the track team all won first place in the conference on the final day of the season. During the middle of the decade men's teams sagged some, but the women's swimming and track teams blossomed with the swimmers winning six state titles and the runners three. Only slightly behind with one first and four seconds came the women gymnasts. Full fledged intercollegiate ice hockey competition started with the 70s and by 1977 under the coaching of Ron Mason Bowling Green was able to enter the first round of the NCAA playoffs. In the years 1977 to 1979 the hockey team finished fifth twice and third once in the NCAA and in early 1979 attained the ranking of the number one hockey team in the nation. One other sport in which the university excelled during the decade, although not quite with the peaks of track, swimming, or ice hockey, was in men's lacrosse. The university glowed, at least vicariously, during the 1980 Winter Olympics when two hockey players, Ken Morrow and Mark Wells, played on the Gold Medal ice hockey team and the town's Scott Hamilton finished fifth in the men's figure skating competition. Finally, at the end of the 1980-81 season the basketball team after thirteen years of frustration finished in a tie for first place.[22]

In addition to the twenty-four intercollegiate sports, athletic opportunities for many other students abounded as well during the 1970s. By 1980 there were eighteen club sports in which both men and women were able to compete intercollegiately at a level that was only slightly lower often than that of the varsity teams. The most successful of these teams consistently was the men's rugby team. During the last half of the decade non-varsity athletic facilities were improved and new ones developed. The two greatest assets added were the improved lighted fields east of Mercer Road and the long awaited Student Recreation Center with its many pools, courts, and other play areas. These facilities permitted a continued expansion of intramural sports which by 1980 included thirty-five sports and involved well over 1400 teams and 12,000 students over the course of a year. On an individual basis largely, students were also using the Rec Center at the rate of 2500 or more participants a day.[23]

As involved as many students were in participating in and watching athletics and in the various recreational activities those were only part of the ongoing life of the student body outside of the classroom.

A Home Away From Home

"Residence halls at Bowling Green State University are designed to play an intergral part in the total educational development of students."[24]

The extensive use of the various recreational facilities was a clear indication of the enduring residential nature of the campus. At the beginning of the 1970s, however, there was considerable question about the continuing viability of on-campus residential housing, but by decade's end over occupancy was a regular occurrence. The early 70s witnessed the opening of the recently named Offenhauer Towers, the last residence hall to be built, and the changing of many long standing policies regarding dormitories.

Interestingly, in spite of the concern about fewer students wanting to live on campus and the opening of Offenhauer, Fall residence hall occcupancy did not fluctutate greatly during the period 1970-1980. The lowest rate occurred in 1972-73 when 7961 were housed and the highest number was in 1980-81 with 8487 living on campus. As early as the 1973-74 academic year overcrowding in the Fall became a problem. Students in the Falls of 1975, 1979, and 1980 also experienced room shortages. This condition while it caused some acrimony at the time did not result in lowered demand for admission to the university or to a mass move to live off campus.[25]

With the opening of Offenhauer in the Fall of 1971 a new differential room charge system was instituted. Three different price levels were created with Offenhauer being the most expensive and the oldest dormitories being the least. The differential for a double was ninety dollars a year. At the same time a new food coupon system was also initiated which ended the flat board charge and replaced it with individually priced items that were paid for by coupons purchased at the start of each quarter. This program was further refined in 1977-78 when three different coupon purchases were made available based on each individuals anticipated number of meals and/or volume of consumption. These options were priced at a rate running from a low of $60 to a high of $127 per quarter. During the course of the decade room and board rates rose an average at the lowest of $606 and the highest $846 for the year or from a total average cost of $1035 to that of $1776 per year.[26]

While some of the rise in costs was inflation related part of it reflected improved housing conditions and more extensive menu selection. In order to make the older residence halls more homelike the university in 1972 spent almost $2 million in improvements. A comparison of a pre-food coupon menu with a post-food coupon menu demonstrates markedly the upgrading that occurred. The breakfast menu did not change appreciably, but the lunch and dinner ones did. A pre-coupon lunch menu offered one soup, two entrees and one vegetable while the post-coupon offering was two soups, five entrees, and two vegetables. The comparable dinner menu was one soup, two entrees, and two vegetables compared to two soups, five entrees and four vegetables. Salad and dessert differentials were similar, plus the post-coupon menu offered ten cold sandwiches and seven hot ones and included the statement "steaks and lobstertail cooked to order upon request." One other food offering feature was the development of specialized food serving areas such as the Berries, the Mid-Am Room, and the Tower Inn.[27]

Starting early in the Moore administration long standing residence hall rules on alcohol were liberalized. In October 1970 *The BG News* trumpeted "Booze barrier busted."[28] The headline followed a 4,2,2 vote of the Board of Trustees by which alcohol useage on campus in accordance with state law was approved. Rules dealing with both private and public consumption were quickly drawn up so that by early 1971 drinking in residence halls and happy hours in the North East Commons and The Nest were ongoing. As the decade passed vandalism became a problem, and led to revising the rules and practices concerning parties and happy hours. By 1979 the North East Commons was no longer used and a year later happy hours in The Nest were limited to three times a quarter.[29]

Simultaneously two other long standing regulations on hours and coed housing were modified. Calls for such changes had permeated much of the unrest of the late 1960s and had been an integral part of the dorm autonomy demands. By 1971 a distinct shift in administrative thinking had occurred partially, at least, caused by the worry over the perceived appeal of off-campus housing. This shift was explicitly stated by the Board of Trustees in March 1972 when it declared:

> "The University commitment to a living-learning concept is evidenced by its extensive building, staff, and programs, in residence halls. Future plans call for increased emphasis on the marriage of academic programs *with a variety of living style options.* Moreover, this emphasis will be increasingly aimed at the growth and needs of freshmen and sophomores through the development of new cluster colleges, innovative teaching methods, student advising, and *greater opportunities for self determination.*"[30]

At the start of the 1971-72 academic year Kreischer Darrow had opened as the first coed residence hall, and set a pattern that was followed for the rest of the decade. In 1972 the first open visitation policy was adopted by which floors and wings could opt for twenty four hour, twelve hour, or lounge only visitation arrangements. After some experimentation various open hour approaches were adopted, but the overall effect was the creation of a more open, resident oriented system than had ever existed before.

A further aspect of the new approach was the development of programming that would enhance the "living-learning concept" of residence life. This was accomplished during the 70s by such techniques as placing heavier emphasis on educational programs versus social; by using individual halls to house the Free University and the various cluster colleges; by establishing a study floor in McDonald East; and by converting Prout Hall into a total educational/cultural coed housing unit.

The broad array of changes in the resident halls raised anew the role, and even the need, for the Association of Women Students whose historic function had been the governing of women's halls. In early 1971 *The BG News* declared editorially "As it exists today, AWS deserves to be abolished."[31] Surprisingly, within a month the organization itself which dated back to 1923 agreed, and voluntarily disbanded at the end of the school year. In time the need for some sort of student involvement in residence life became clear, and so in the Fall of 1975 a campus wide, inter-living hall organization was formed called variously the Residence Hall Association, the Residence Life Association, and the Residence Student Association. The organization concerned itself largely with the communication of ideas between buildings, the development of rules, and the general quality of dormitory life.[32]

While on-campus housing was of greater concern to the administration off-campus facilities had considerable impact as well. The hope and planning for a Greek Village continued through the first year of the Moore Administration. In May 1971, however, the university was informed that the plans had been placed on hold—a decision that proved to be permanent. During 1971 and 1972 a recurrent theme in town-gown relations resurfaced; namely, the condition of student housing. A proposed housing code and rental licensing ordinance was heatedly debated with the landlords generally opposing it and the students advocating its enactment. The final outcome was slight, but the issue was to resurface again a decade later.[33]

Even though Bowling Green had approximately three-fifths of the student body residing on campus another 6000 did not. Historically the bond that tied these two groups together was the student government.

To Be Or Not To Be?
Student Government During The Moore Years

When President Moore assumed office university governance was in a seeming state of flux. One of the major questions concerned the degree to which students should be involved, and how that involvement should be integrated into the total governance structure. Traditionally, a dual system of student involvement had existed. There had been a student council/senate which represented most clearly student interests, but students had served extensively, as well, on innumerable university committees and councils.

The student emphasis in 1970 was to create some sort of community council which would deal with all the broad matters of university policy, and upon which student representation would be considerable. For three years the university community—faculty, students, and administration—vacillated between various approaches. Finally, in May 1973 President Moore established the Committee on University Governance and Reorganization from which, as already seen, The Academic Charter of 1976 evolved. That document formalized the inclusion of student representatives in the Faculty Senate, but also the duality of a student council and a faculty body. Tradition and the new charter resulted in the continuation, therefore, of a student body organization.

While reorganization of university governance consumed six years, the resolution of the role of student government engulfed the entire Moore administration and was still unresolved at its end. During the decade from 1971 to 1981 four separate student government constitutions were adopted; three of which differed largely only in the organizational structure provided. The differing views of governance and the subsequent indecision and lack of action led The BG News in 1977 to assert: "It is time to form a student government with real power and the ability to work together. Striving for anything less than that is simply inviting continued mediocrity."[34] That feeling of frustration and apparent powerlessness no doubt was reflected in the voting turnout for student goverment elections. For elections held during the 70s the average student electors composed only eight and a half percent of the eligible voters. The situation degenerated to the point that in 1980 the News headed an editorial "Of apathy and disillusionment"[35] when it was announced that elections were being delayed because forty-two percent of the offices to be filled had either one or no candidates on the ballot. In the

Spring of 1981 the plight had reached the point where elections were deferred to the Fall and the *News* once again editorialized "Will there be an SGA? Does anyone care?"[36]

That the student body organization, while important, was not the only means by which the student body could express itself was clearly enunciated by the Board of Trustees at its meeting of January 8, 1971. In a joint statement with the Student Council it was pointed out that students served on forty one university and college councils and committees. Additionally, at the meeting final agreement was reached on having an undergraduate student representative meet regularly with the Board. This privilege was extended in January 1976 to include a graduate student representative, as well. A further major involvement of students commenced in the Fall of 1972 when President Moore approved the creation of what became known as the Advisory Committee on General Fee Allocations. The committee composed primarily of students was given the initial responsibility for recommending the budget allocations for all groups receiving General Fee monies. The importance of this committee grew sufficiently so that by 1980 controversy erupted among various student groups as to the basis and equity of the student membership, as appointed by the Student Government Association. Consequently, Provost Ferrari reorganized the committee so that the various student interests on campus would be represented.[37]

Student involvement in another area proved to be equally controversial although in this case the strain was between students and the faculty. In the Fall of 1970 the Academic Council adopted a policy which required in cases of promotion and special merit raises the use of student evaluations as part of the supporting evidence. Faculty reaction varied, but there was considerable disagreement concerning both the requirement and the statistical reliability of teacher evaluation instruments. The student body organization gave much support to the use of evaluation forms, but as the decade wore on their actual use by departments tended to decline. In 1976 the College of Business faculty voted overwhelmingly to discontinue the then mandatory use of them in the college.[38]

The Moore Years - 1970-1981
Hollis A. Moore, Jr. - The Man And His Presidency

In late February 1981 Hollis Moore entered the Medical College of Ohio Hospital in Toledo for treatment through a com-
bination of radiation therapy and rest of a "low malignancy"
brain tumor. Two months later he was dead. While for several
years President Moore had been incapacitated for short periods
of time by recurring health problems attributed to
myelofibrosis, his sudden decline in 1981 was a shock to most
people at the university. The severity of his problem was at least
partially foretold when the Board of Trustees on March 12th officially authorized Provost Michael Ferrari to act as president
during the absence of Moore. The death of President Moore
evoked many expressions of appreciation, both official and personal, for his years of service to Bowling Green. Among them
were official resolutions from the Board of Trustees, the Faculty Senate, and the Student Body Organization. In addition,
the Student Body Organization established a special Hollis A.
Moore University Service Award to be given annually and the
Trustees unanimously voted to name the new music building
The Hollis and Marian Moore Musical Arts Center.[39] His role
and contribution to the university and higher education were
well summarized in the Faculty Senate Resolution which said in
part:

> "He touched all of us in his dedication to excellence for the in-
> stitution, always in terms of the human dimension. Both by act
> and by example, he fostered concern for the intellectual, the
> moral, the cultural, and the physical development of the com-
> munity. These attributes have been made manifest in his open
> style of administration, in enhancing the residential character of
> the University, in providing our students an international dimen-
> sion, and in implementing the development of new programs.

> He made distinguished contributions in championing education
> at national, state and local levels. At the national level, this
> achievement is typified by the time-flexible degree program and
> by his distinguished service on the Board of Directors of the
> American Association of State Colleges and Universities. Within
> the National Collegiate Athletic Association he urged re-

examination of expenditures and ethical standards for inter-collegiate athletics.

He was a vigorous advocate on behalf of higher education in the State of Ohio. His contributions are represented by leadership roles within the Inter-University Council, the Ohio College Association, and the Council of Presidents of the Mid-American Athletic Conference.

In Northwest Ohio his service on the Board of Directors of both the Greater Toledo Community Chest and the Toledo Symphony Orchestra Society exemplified his concern for the role of the University beyond the campus. Moreover, he was instrumental in the development of inter-institutional academic programs and centers.

For the University, his vision found realization in the Musical Arts Center and the Student Recreation Center, in his promotion of scholarships for academic excellence, and in the enhancement of the multicultural character of campus life.

For us, his moral integrity, his creativity, his sense of style, his flair for living, his lively intellectual curiosity, and his friendly manner are an enduring legacy. His hope, as expressed in his first address to the faculty, for a Decade of Distinction at Bowling Green State University has been richly fulfilled and will continue as an inspiration to each of us.''[40]

Even the eulogies for Hollis Moore did not touch on all of his virtues and, as is customary, ignored his failings. While his shortcomings were few, he had some. His temper was short particularly when it concerned athletics, but also when individuals in whom he had placed confidence failed to perform up to expectations. He was prone, especially in his first years as president, to be overly impressed by people who seemed exceptionally energetic and creative. He tended to be somewhat impatient; a trait which reflected itself in his unwillingness to bother with details or to invest, often, interminable time in working out a problem. He was usually gentlemanly in his dealings with individuals, but upon occasion he could be acid in his remarks and letters. All of this is to say, that Hollis Moore was human.

Increasingly during the last few months of President Moore's life the Provost, Michael R. Ferrari and the Vice President and Secretary of the Board, Richard A. Edwards ran the university.

It was only natural then that following President Moore's death the Board of Trustees would turn to them. The Board at its meeting of May 8, 1981 appointed Ferrari, Interim President, and Edwards, Executive Vice President, thus making them the top two administrative officers of the university. Shortly, thereafter the Board moved to create a Presidential Search Committee composed of Board members, administrators, faculty, students, and alumni.[41]

Notes

Chapter V

1. *BOT Min.,* July 10, 1970. James Bond To Board.

2. *BGN,* Vol. 55, #22, Oct. 7, 1970, p. 1, #27, Oct. 14, 1970, p. 1, #33, Oct. 22, 1970, p. 1, #39, Oct. 30, 1970, p. 1, #43, Nov. 5, 1970, p.1.

3. *Ibid.,* #127, May 19, 1971, p. 1.

4. *BOT Min.* May 20, 1971; *BGN,* Vol. 55, #116, April 29, 1971, pp. 1&3, #117, April 30, 1971, p. 2, #118, May 4, 1971, p. 1, #119, May 5, 1971, pp. 1&2, #120, May 6, 1971, p. 1, #121, May 7, 1971, pp. 1&2, #123, May 12, 1971, p. 1, #124, May 13, 1971, p. 1, #126, May 18, 1971, pp. 1&2, #127, May 19, 1971, p. 1, #128, May 20, 1971, p. 1, #129, May 21, 1971, p. 2, #130, May 25, 1971, p. 1, #133, May 28, 1971, p. 1, #134, June 2, 1971, pp. 1&2, & #136, June 4, 1971, p. 1.

5. *Ibid,* Vol. 56, #40, Nov. 19, 1971, p. 2.

6. *Ibid,* #89, March 31, 1972, p. 2.

7. *Ibid,* #21, Oct. 19, 1971, p. 1, #47, Dec. 8, 1971, p. 1, #50, Jan. 7, 1972, p. 1, #54, Jan. 14, 1972, p. 1, #88, March 30, 1972, p. 1, #92, April 6, 1972, p. 1, #104, April 27, 1972, p. 1, #109, May 5, 1972, p. 1, #111, May 10, 1972, pp. 1&2, #112, May 11, 1972, p. 1, #125, June 2, 1972, p. 1, & #130, July 27, 1972, p. 1.

8. *Ibid.,* #125, June 21, 1973, p. 1, #126, June 28, 1973, p. 1, Vol. 57, #3, July 19, 1973, pp. 1 & 2, #4, July 26, 1973, p. 1, #86, March 27, 1974, p. 1, Vol. 58, #36, Nov. 8, 1974, p. 1, #44, Nov. 22, 1974, p. 5; *CAC-HAM,* Box 32, Folder 2.

9. *BGN,* Vol. 58, #48, Jan. 8, 1975, p. 1, #58, Jan. 24, 1975, pp. 2 & 5, #68, Feb. 7, 1975, p. 1, #73, Feb. 14, 1975, p. 1, #127, May 20, 1975, pp. 1 & 3, #128, May 21, 1975, p. 2, Vol. 59, #109, May 6, 1976, p. 1, Vol. 60, #7, Sept. 9, 1976, pp. 1 & 2, #27, Nov. 4, 1976, p. 2, #51, Jan. 19, 1977, p. 1, #92, April 15, 1977, p. 1, #95, April 21, 1977, p. 3, #100, April 29, 1977, p. 1, #105, May 10, 1977, p. 1, Vol. 61, #14, Oct. 12, 1977, p. 1, #24, Oct. 28, 1977, p. 1, #31, Nov. 10, 1977, p. 1, #32, Nov. 11, 1977, pp. 1 & 2, #107, May 23, 1978, p. 1; *BOT Min.,* April 14, 1977, May 12, 1977, Nov. 10, 1977, Jan. 18, 1979, and Aug. 9, 1979.

10. *BGN,* Vol. 64, #282, May 25, 1979, p. 1, #283, May 30, 1979, pp. 1 & 3, #284, May 31, 1979, p. 1, Vol. 65, #11, Oct. 11, 1979, p. 1, #26, Nov. 8, 1979, p. 1, #32, Nov. 27, 1979, p. 1, #37, Dec. 5, 1979, p. 1, #55, Feb. 1, 1980, p. 1, #86, April 15, 1980, p. 1, #100, May 8, 1980, p. 3; *BOT Min.,* Oct. 11, 1979.

11. *BGN,* Vol. 65, #99, May 7, 1980, p. 1, #100, May 8, 1980, p. 1, #101, May 9, 1980, p. 1, #102, May 13, 1980, p. 1, #110, May 28, 1980, pp. 1 & 7, #113, June 3, 1980, p. 1, #125, Aug. 21, 1980, pp. 1 & 6, Vol. 66, #3, Sept. 26, 1980, pp. 1 & 8, #32, Nov. 18, 1980, p. 1, Vol. 61, #68, Feb. 25, 1981, p. 1.

12. *CAC-HAM,* Box 32, Folder 69. President's Address to 1971 Freshmen.

13. *Ibid.,* Box 33, Folder 158, p. 4; *BGN,* Vol. 55, #25, Oct. 13, 1970, p. 6, #29, Oct. 16, 1970, p. 5, #131, May 27, 1971, p. 1, Vol. 58, #33, Nov. 5, 1974, p. 1.

14. *BGN,* Vol. 58, #34, June 3, 1975, pp. 1 & 2.

Notes

Chapter V (cont'd.)

15. *BOT Min.,* Dec. 16, 1971; MS-449, Interview with Richard Eakin; *BGN,* Vol. 56, #32, Nov. 5, 1971, p. 1, #33, Nov. 9, 1971, p. 1, #51, Jan. 11, 1972, p. 1, #59, Jan. 25, 1972, p. 1, #60, Jan. 26, 1972, p. 1, #61, Jan. 27, 1972, p. 1, Vol. 56, #24, Oct. 20, 1972, p. 1, #25, Oct. 24, 1972, p. 2, #104, April 27, 1973, p. 1, #106, May 2, 1973, p. 1, #118, May 23, 1973, p. 1, Vol. 57, #17, Oct. 10, 1973, p. 1, Vol. 58, #34, June 3, 1975, pp. 1 & 2.

16. *BOT Min.,* Oct. 24, 1972, Nov. 15, 1976, Sept. 30, 1977, Oct. 11, 1979, Jan. 10, 1980; *BGN,* Vol. 56, #6, Sept. 20, 1971, p. 13, #90, April 4, 1972, p. 2, Vol. 56, #26, Oct. 25, 1972, p. 1, #72, Feb. 15, 1973, p. 1, #112, May 11, 1973, p. 1, Vol. 57, #9, Sept. 26, 1973, p. 1, #26, Oct. 25, 1973, p. 1, Vol. 58, #17, Oct. 8, 1974, p. 1, #24, Oct. 18, 1974, p. 1, & Vol. 61, #9, Oct. 4, 1977, p. 1.

17. *BGN,* Vol. 61, #54, Feb. 1, 1978, pp. 1-4, #55, Feb. 2, 1978, pp. 1-3, #56, Feb. 3, 1978, pp. 1-3, #57, Feb. 7, 1978, pp. 1-2, & #58, Feb. 8, 1978, pp. 1-2.

18. *BOT Min.,* Jan. 10, 1980; *BGN,* Vol. 56, #32, Nov. 5, 1971, p. 1, Vol. 58, #23, Oct. 17, 1974, p. 1, #27, Oct. 24, 1974, p. 1, Vol. 61, #45, Jan. 12, 1978, p. 5; *The 1981 Key,* pp. 29-33.

19. *BGN,* Vol. 56, #19, Oct. 14, 1975, p. 1, Vol. 59, #19, Oct. 25, 1975, p. 1, #47, Jan. 21, 1976, p. 1, Vol. 61, #72, March 3, 1978, p. 1, #108, May 24, 1978, p. 3, Vol. 65, #80, April 3, 1980, pp. 1, 2, & 7, #81, April 4, 1980, pp. 1-2, #84, April 10, 1980, p. 1, #85, April 11, 1980, p. 1, #86, April 15, 1980, p. 1, #89, April 18, 1980, p. 1, #90, April 22, 1980, p. 1, & #100, May 8, 1980, p. 1.

20. *Ibid. [BGN],* Vol. 55, #23, Oct. 8, 1970, p. 1.

21. *CAC-HAM,* Box 32, Folder 136; *BOT Min.,* Jan. 8, 1971, May 20, 1971, March 11, 1976, April 8, 1976, May 13, 1976, Feb. 10, 1977; *BGN,* Vol. 58, #49, Jan. 9, 1975, p. 1, #73, Feb. 14, 1975, p. 1, Vol. 59, #72, Feb. 17, 1976, p. 1, #97, April 15, 1976, p. 1, #126, June 4, 1976, p. 1, Vol. 60, #38, Nov. 23, 1976, p. 1, #43, Jan. 5, 1977, p. 1, Vol. 65, #39, Dec. 7, 1979, p. 10.

22. *BOT Min.,* Oct. 24, 1972, April 13, 1978, April 24, 1980; *MS-376,* #12; Moyers, *All Sports,* passim; *BGN,* Vol. 61, #217, Jan. 16, 1979, p. 1.

23. Wilson, *Intramural,* pp. 106, 127, & 128; *BOT Min.,* May 3, 1973, Aug. 16, 1973, Jan. 9, 1975, May 15, 1975, March 11, 1976, Oct. 11, 1979; *Bulletin,* 1981-83, p. 29; *BGN.,* Vol. 56, #108, May 4, 1973, p. 1.

24. *MS-376,* #4d. Board of Trustees "Statement on Residence Halls."

25. *BGN,* Vol. 57, #10, Sept. 29, 1973, p. 1, Vol. 59, #16, Oct. 21, 1975, p. 1, #23, Oct. 31, 1975, p. 1, Vol. 65, #1, Sept. 23, 1979, p. 1, #2, Sept. 26, 1979, pp. 1 & 4, #125, Aug. 21, 1980, pp. 1 & 4, Vol. 66, #1, Sept. 21, 1980, pp. 1, 10-11, #22, Oct. 30, 1980, pp. 1 & 4.

26. *MS-376,* #4 & 4d.

27. *Ibid.,* #4c; *BOT Min.,* Feb. 24, 1972.

28. *BGN,* Vol. 55, #21, Oct. 6, 1970, p. 1.

Notes

Chapter V (cont'd.)

29. *BOT Min.,* Oct. 2, 1970, April 19, 1979; Elsbrock, *Residence Life,* pp. 133-35; *BGN,* Vol. 55, #21, Oct. 6, 1970, p. 1, #28, Oct. 15, 1970, p. 1, #48, Nov. 12, 1970, p. 1, Vol. 57, #113, May 14, 1974, p. 1, Vol. 58, #100, April 10, 1975, p. 1, Vol. 61, #14, Oct. 12, 1977, p. 3, Vol. 65, #43, Jan. 11, 1980, p. 1, Vol. 66, #4, Sept. 30, 1980, p. 1, #13, Oct. 15, 1980, p. 1.

30. *MS-376,* #4d; *BOT Min.,* March 18, 1972. (Emphasis added by author.)

31. *BGN,* Vol. 55, #66, Jan. 13, 1971, p. 2.

32. Elsbrock, *Residence Life,* pp. 58, 60-1, 67-8, 72-6, 102-05, 113-19, 122-27, 139-40; *BOT Min.,* Dec. 16, 1971, March 18, 1972, June 2, 1972, Oct. 24, 1972, Nov. 6, 1975, Sept. 30, 1977, & March 12, 1981; *BGN,* Vol. 55, #44, Nov. 6, 1970, p. 1, #63, Jan. 7, 1971, p. 1, #66, Jan. 13, 1971, p. 2, #67, Jan. 14, 1971, p. 2, #89, Feb. 24, 1971, p. 1, #103, April 6, 1971, p. 1, Vol. 56, #24, Oct. 22, 1971, pp. 1 & 5, Vol. 56, #9, Sept. 24, 1972, p. 4, #22, Oct. 18, 1972, p. 1, #111, May 10, 1973, p. 1, Vol. 59, #11, Oct. 9, 1975, p. 1, & #30, Nov. 13, 1975, p. 1.

33. *BOT Min.,* July 10, 1970, Feb. 5, 1971, March 10, 1971, & May 20, 1971; *BGN,* Vol. 55, #25, Oct. 13, 1970, p. 1, #72, Jan. 22, 1971, p. 3, #78, Feb. 3, 1971, p. 3, #91, Feb. 26, 1971, p. 1, #103, April 6, 1971, p. 1, Vol. 56, #11, Sept. 30, 1971, p. 1, & #26, Oct. 25, 1972, pp. 1-2.

34. *BGN,* Vol. 60, #75, March 2, 1977, p. 2.

35. *Ibid.,* Vol. 65, #78, March 13, 1980, p. 2.

36. *Ibid.,* Vol. 66, #78, April 15, 1981, p. 2. Also: Vol. 54, #107, May 20, 1970, p. 1, #111, May 27, 1970, p. 1, #113, May 29, 1970, p. 1, Vol. 55, #21, Oct. 6, 1970, p. 1, #25, Oct. 13, 1970, p. 1, #36, Oct. 27, 1970, p. 1, #43, Nov. 5, 1970, p. 1, #53, Nov. 19, 1970, p. 1, Vol. 56, #6, Sept. 26, 1971, p. 7, #17, Oct. 12, 1971, p. 1, #61, Jan. 22, 1972, p. 1, #63, Feb. 1, 1972, p. 1, Vol. 60, #74, March 1, 1977, p. 1, #79, March 9, 1977, p. 1, Vol. 61, #75, March 9, 1978, p. 1, Vol. 65, #78, March 13, 1980, p. 2, Vol. 66, #68, Feb. 25, 1981, pp. 1-2, #77, April 14, 1981, p. 1, & #80, April 17, 1981, p. 1.

37. *BOT Min.,* Jan. 8, 1971, Jan. 6, 1976, & Feb. 12, 1976; *BGN,* Vol. 55, #42, Nov. 4, 1970, p. 1, #46, Nov. 10, 1970, pp. 1-2, #65, Jan. 12, 1971, p. 1, Vol. 56, #70, Feb. 11, 1972, p. 1, #133, Aug. 17, 1972, p. 1, Vol. 56, #13, Oct. 3, 1972, p. 1, Vol. 59, #71, Feb. 13, 1976, pp. 1-2, Vol. 65, #81, p. 3, & #125, Aug. 21, 1980, pp. 1 & 6.

38. *CAC-Comm. & Councils,* Box 6, Acad Council, Dec. 2, 1970; *CAC-Fac Sen Coll,* Box 11, Attached to Min. of Feb. 2, 1971; *BGN,* Vol. 54, #124, July 9, 1970, p. 1, Vol. 55, #51, Nov. 17, 1970, p. 1, Vol. 56, #60, Jan. 26, 1972, p. 1, & Vol. 59, #77, Feb. 25, 1976, pp. 2-3.

39. *BOT Min.,* March 12, 1981, May 8, 1981; *BGN,* Vol. 61, #72, 1981, p. 1, #79, April 2, 1981, p. 3, #81, April 21, 1981, p. 1.

40. *CAC-Fac Sen Coll,* Box 26-A, Folder 4.

41. *BOT Min.,* May 8, 1981; *MS-376,* #44, Interview with Richard A. Edwards; *BGN,* Vol. 61, #93, May 12, 1981, p. 1.

The Campus — 1985

NCAA Hockey Champions — Lake Placid, N.Y. — March, 1984

SECTION IV

Surprise, Controversy, and New Directions

Michael R. Ferrari
Interim President — 1981-1982

CHAPTER VI
Bowling Green in the 1980s

Paul J. Olscamp
President — 1982-

156

CHAPTER VI

Bowling Green in the 1980s

For eleven months the process of selecting a successor for Hollis Moore kept the campus in suspense and a certain degree of turmoil. At the May, 1981 meeting of the Board of Trustees, the Chair, Frazier Reams, Jr., appointed a committee instructed to establish procedures and a time table for selecting a president. A month later the Board appointed a Presidential Search and Screening Committee which was guided by the report of the prior committee, although its provisions were not made public. Dissatisfaction with the seeming "secrecy" of the entire process surfaced by the Fall and led the Faculty Senate in October to pass a resolution which expressed its unhappiness with the decision to keep "...all information regarding procedures and selection criteria confidential."[1] The Senate further called upon the Board to adjust its policy and allow the dissemination of information in those areas where it would not discourage the candidacy of anyone. A few days later the Board refused to change its policy. On March 15, 1982 Board Chair Frazier Reams, Jr. announced, at a press conference, the appointment of Paul J. Olscamp as the eighth president of Bowling Green State University, and stated that he would officially assume office on July 1. When that day arrived, Michael R. Ferrari, who had served as Interim President for fourteen months, stepped aside and assumed the position of Trustee Professor of Administration.[2]

The Administration of Michael R. Ferrari

"The financial uncertainties and pressures facing Bowling Green State University have never been greater in its 71-year history."[3]

157

Much of the time and energy of Michael Ferrari during his year as Interim President was invested in dealing with a series of financial crises and attending matters. His address to the faculty and staff at the opening of school in September, 1981 was devoted almost exclusively to the fiscal distress of the university and to proposed ways of dealing with it. The misery was a clear reflection of the economic plight of the state. By the Fall of 1981 the university had experienced a decline over three years of twenty eight percent in state subsidy support, and faced an anticipated budget deficit of $1.3 million for the ensuing academic year. Many solutions were proposed, and various of them were implemented. The most far reaching remedy was taken unilaterally by the Board of Trustees in July with the decision to convert the academic calendar from the quarter system to an early semester one; a move that it was estimated would save $35,000 or more in administrative costs. While many of the faculty objected to the method followed, the severity of the financial crisis muted the outcry considerably. During the early Fall, the belt tightening of the past three years was extended further by such means as continued hiring freezes, the elimination of some positions, the cutting of some selected budgets, and increased efforts at improved productivity.

Late in the Fall and into the early beginnings of 1982 the state economy seemed to be improving. During that period the legislature approved capital funds for both a physical sciences laboratory building and a biological sciences laboratory annex at a cost of $8.2 million, and also finally released a payment of $3 million for the aquatic portion of the Student Recreation Center. As suddenly as the economic picture had brightened it turned again to gloom. In late January the governor revealed that the state was faced with a $1 billion dollar deficit, and ordered an immediate 8.9% budget cut for the rest of the 1982 fiscal year and 16.3% for the 1983 fiscal year. The 1982 cut had the effect of slicing actually a little over 20% from the money left for Fiscal Year 1982. This new juncture led the administration to order a series of rather Draconian budget slashes, such as the lapsing of all operating contingency reserves, a 25% cut in unencumbered operating budgets in non-instructional areas and of 10% in instructional ones, a stop on all new proposed funding, a freeze on all travel, and some dozen more moves of a similar sort. The other major response was a reluctant, but necessary sharp increase both for 1981-82 and 1982-83 of the instructional fees.[4]

The length of the Ferrari presidency coupled with the overwhelming fiscal problems limited the amount of progress. In addition, the very interim nature of the appointment placed restraints on initiating new plans. It was ironic, therefore, that when the opportunity to act presented itself, Ferrari was not able to carry out his conviction that the 1980s were a "Time to be bold."[5] Even so, the university did move ahead. Several significant academic steps were taken that strengthened the teaching, research, and service components of the university. During the year the Acting Provost, John Eriksen, proposed and the Faculty Senate approved the creation of both special teaching and special research professorships which would recognize outstanding achievement in one of those two areas. The Alumni Association also moved to recognize exceptional teaching by giving its first Master Teacher Award in the Spring of 1982. The importance of research and service were clearly denoted with the official formation of two new centers—one for Social Philosophy and Policy and one for Population and Social Research. Another development of direct value to students as well as faculty and staff was the opening in the Fall of 1981 of a new microcomputer lab in West Hall, which absorbed most of the demand of both Basic and Fortran computer classes. The financial crunch was partially responsible for one other advance; namely, the inauguration of a one day interlibrary loan service between Bowling Green and the University of Toledo — a cooperative venture that immediately increased appreciably the library resources of both institutions.[6]

As mentioned earlier, during the 1981-82 academic year the university received some funds for capital improvements; the first such money in five years. As a result, in June and July of 1982 construction was begun on the physical and biological sciences buildings. The summer before, a fifty five foot tall carillon bell tower, a gift of the Classes of 1975, 1976, and 1978, was erected on the mall between the Education Building and the Library. In the Spring of 1982 the Board of Trustees also ap-

proved the capital improvements request for the next three bienniums. Additionally, the Board approved the naming of the
university golf course in honor of the longtime golf coach, For-
rest Creason.[7]

The Interim And The Students

As school opened in the Fall of 1981 the enrollment on campus stood at 17,018 with an FTE of 16,335. Of the enrollees,
8,064 were housed on campus. Both the enrollment and the
number housed on campus were a planned decrease from the
previous year. The former aimed at meeting the demand from
the Board of Regents to bring enrollment in line with the
legislatively mandated 15,000 FTE, and the latter to end the
problems and discontent arising from the residence hall overcrowding of the years immediately preceding. The distribution
of students registered among the colleges reflected the changing
career options of students. The College of Business had the
most students with 4639 of whom forty five percent were
women, followed by the College of Arts and Sciences with 4057,
and third the College of Education with 3487. While enrollment
remained high, the changing demographic patterns led the administration to move forward the opening application date in
the hope of getting individuals to commit themselves earlier to
attend, and thus maintain the enrollment level.[8]

The greatest excitement during the year 1981-82 centered
around the proposed new constitution for the Student Government Association, and especially on that part which asserted the
"right to have input into, access to, justification for all decisions concerning financial, academic, and social affairs involving the general welfare of the student body."[9] The Faculty
Senate at its meeting of October 6, 1981 by a vote of 50-5 objected to the inclusion of students on committees dealing with
promotion, salaries, and tenure. The *BG News* responded
editorially to the vote saying "Faculty Senate seems to think
that it is a privilege for students to sit on committees. We believe
it is a right."[10] When the student body was asked to approve the
proposed constitution twenty percent of them turned out (the
highest percentage in over a decade), and voted overwhelmingly

in favor of it. In November the Board of Trustees approved on an interim basis, with the exception of the powers objected to by the Faculty Senate, the constitution of the renamed Undergraduate Student Government. With that, attitudes quickly returned to normal so that by early January of 1982 the *BG News* was bemoaning the fact that only a few students had indicated an interest in running for student government.[11]

1981-82 was a seemingly paradoxical one athletically. As a result of the financial dilemma the Athletic Director, James Lessig, in February announced that the university was dropping from varsity status men's wrestling, women's field hockey, and men and women's indoor track. While there was considerable furor the decision stood. Yet, two months later the university informed the NCAA that it was in the process of increasing the stadium capacity by more than 4000 seats. The latter action was necessitated by the desire of the university and the Mid-American Conference to maintain Division 1-A status in football, and, therefore, was partially financed by member schools of the conference.[12]

The Changing of the Guard

"The past eleven years have been for me and my family exceedingly rich."

"I am not interpreting this whole thing as anti-Olscamp, because I'm sure people were emotional about losing a popular leader."[13]

The announcement of the selection of Paul J. Olscamp as the eighth president of Bowling Green State University caused considerable turmoil. The negative reaction centered on the Board of Trustees which was charged with being high-handed and not in "touch with the feelings of the university."[14] The first public outcry came in a rare editorial on March 22, 1982 in *The Daily Sentinel-Tribune* of Bowling Green which severely criticized the Board of Trustees. It called upon its readers to carry on a "massive" letter writing campaign asking the Board to reconsider its decision before it had to confirm it officially at its public meeting on April 9th. A few days later the Chair of the Faculty Senate circulated a copy of the editorial to everyone at the university "for your consideration and, hopefully, your action."[15] On April 6th a general faculty meeting was held at which approximately half of the faculty were in attendance. At the meeting two resolutions were adopted one of which commended Ferrari for his service and congratulated Olscamp on his appointment. The other sharply criticized the Trustees for their "growing disposition to act unilaterally and in isolation," which had resulted in "a dramatic erosion of mutual trust and respect" between them and the faculty.[16] A similar set of resolutions was passed by the Undergraduate Student Government. All of the resolutions were presented to the Board on April 9th at which meeting the appointment of Paul J. Olscamp as President was affirmed. The newly elected President acknowledged publicly the strain which existed within the university, but insisted that it was a problem between the faculty and students on the one hand and the Trustees on the other and not between himself and either group. Following his appearance in early April, Olscamp returned periodically until he officially assumed office on July 1, 1982.[17]

The man who assumed the presidency was a forty-four year old who had been serving for the previous seven years as President of Western Washington University. Born and raised in Canada, he had earned his B.A. and M.A. degrees at the University of Western Ontario, and his Ph.D. in philosophy at the University of Rochester. Even though he had over ten years of administrative experience when he arrived, he had remained active as a scholar with a number of books and articles to his credit.

Old Foundations - New Directions

President Olscamp described a university as at least:

> "An association of otherwise diverse professionals, with different backgrounds, different training, and different interests, often with very different personalities; A storehouse for the accumulated knowledge of society; A physical center for the performance of research; A knowledge transmission center; A social development center for young people; An opinion formation center; and a counterweight to rapid social change."[18]

Using his description of a university, President Olscamp declared that Bowling Green fit his model generally. The soundness of the university as it entered this new phase of its history was reflected in its acceptance by national honor and accrediting organizations. In August 1982 the university was accepted as a sheltering institution for a chapter of Phi Beta Kappa. In 1983 the School of Technology was accredited and all of the undergraduate programs of the College of Business were reaccredited by their respective national associations. Additionally, the academic programs of the entire university were reaccredited for ten years by the North Central Association of Colleges and Schools. Further recognition came in the Fall of 1983 when the 143 member National Association of State Universities and Land Grant Colleges accepted Bowling Green as a member. One other major reaccreditation occurred in 1984 when all of the teacher-education programs in the College of Education were reconfirmed by the National Council of Accreditation for Teacher Education. Acknowledging this foundation, the new President averred, however, that "...we must improve our academic reputation and performance, for in the long run the institutions that will survive and prosper...are those which are committed to quality..."[19]

Early in the Fall of 1982 President Olscamp in an address to faculty, staff, and students disclosed many of his ideas for the university. He indicated his hope that his proposals would indicate his commitment to "...excellence and to making myself, our university and our community a qualitatively better place to be and to work."[20] His directional outline encompassed academic, personnel, governance, and student areas. He suggested that the academic atmosphere could be improved if superior teaching and research were rewarded more fully, and if fair standards for differential teaching loads were developed. He advocated a revamping of the Academic Charter so as to separate basic faculty rights and functions from contractual, policy, and procedural concerns. As a part of the revamping he supported giving the Faculty Senate an increased role in curricular and budgetary affairs. Finally, he sketched out a variety of approaches geared at maintaining enrollment stability.[21]

Further amplification of his educational philosophy came in two addresses to the faculty that were delivered in October, 1983 and February, 1984. In the former speech he offered his views on the role and mission of the university in fully educating the undergraduate student. The major thrust of his argument was the responsibility to provide all students a broader, but integrated understanding of the world in which they live and of the ways one goes about understanding it. In the February presentation the President devoted himself to graduate education and faculty research, and was much more pragmatic in his approach. He indicated his desire to increase the graduate enrollment from 1900 FTE to 3000 FTE over a period of time and, consequently, lower the undergraduate numbers so as to remain within the 15,000 FTE mandated by law. This change of emphasis would entail, he asserted, the need to provide numerous modifications in teaching loads, financial support, and research expectations. After a little more than a year of his arrival, President Olscamp had made clear his educational philosophy, and had begun the process of persuasion and, where feasible, implementation.[22]

Improving the Old - Building Anew

During the first three and a half years of his presidency, Dr. Olscamp in conjunction with the Board of Trustees, the faculty and staff, and the students accomplished many of the goals he had set. Many of these were intended to improve or adjust patterns and policies already in place —improving the old, while others were designed to enhance future development—building anew. The first major change was inherited with the assumption of the presidency; namely, the initiation of the early semester calendar in August, 1982. While the conversion from the quarter system was not trouble free—one administrator wrote, it did create, among other things, "an exacerbation of existing resource inadequacies"[23] — the transition generally was successful. The first alteration taken by the President was to revamp the administrative organization by placing a Vice President in charge of each functional area—academic affairs, student affairs, operations, and university relations. In May, 1983 a fifth area and Vice Presidency was created; that of planning and budgeting.[24]

Several academic and governance measures were instituted in 1982-83. At his first board meeting officially as President,

Olscamp persuaded the Trustees to allow the faculty and student representatives to the Board to sit with the Finance and the Personnel and Facilities Committees when they met. In December, 1982 the President formed a Charter Revision Committee and named Betty van der Smissen, Vice Chair of the Faculty Senate, to head it. In the Fall the President also proposed to the Faculty Senate that the proportion of salary increments for merit be increased to forty percent of the whole. By the Spring of 1983 the Faculty Senate was presented with a revamped charter and a revised salary formula, and after much debate adopted both. The revised Academic Charter accomplished the division that the President had called for, and also increased the role of the Faculty Senate in the academic and budget domains by creating as committees of the Senate, the Undergraduate Council and the Faculty Senate Budget Committee, both of which had general jurisdiction in the areas delegated to them. Furthermore, the Senate adopted a financial exigency plan which assured an orderly process for dealing with faculty/staff reductions in the case of a substantial economic crisis.[25]

During the Academic Year 1983-84 there evolved several forward looking developments. The biggest project undertaken and completed was that of the Commission on the Role and Mission of the University. The study was a massive undertaking involving the active participation on eight different subcommittees of a couple hundred faculty, staff, and students who examined all aspects of the role and mission of Bowling Green, both contemporaneously and in the future. The final statement set forth twenty seven separate goals within four general categories; 1. Constituencies (areas and people served), 2. Academic Programs (programs and degree options), 3. Learning Environments (research, curriculum, and student development), and 4. Faculty and Resources (faculty and facility improvement, library enrichment, and faculty morale). President Olscamp characterized the Role and Mission Statement to the Trustees as "...the most important and well-justified policy change for this University in the last 15 years."[26] Even though the role and mission effort dominated the year there were other developments of significance. High among these was the creation in August, 1983 of a Task Force on Computing which was directed to expand and upgrade the computational capabilities and services of the university. The move was partially necessitated by the withdrawal of Bowling Green from a frustrating ten-year experience as part of the JPLRCC Consortium in Perrysburg. Over the first two years, aided by some extra state financing, a substantial increase in the quality of services and the availability of various types of computers was achieved. These steps encouraged the university to believe that within another student generation all baccalaureate graduates would be computer literate.[27]

Several policies and projects that had been debated for some time reached a culmination during 1984-85. After several years of study and innumerable revisions, the Faculty Senate in November, 1984 adopted a University General Education Policy which laid "...the foundation of Bowling Green State University's emphasis on a practical liberal education for all undergraduate students."[28] The policy guaranteed that all students would experience courses in the functional areas of Foreign Languages and Multicultural Studies, Social Sciences, Natural Sciences, and Humanities and Arts. Moreover, the policy declared that "...each course must emphasize the development and enhancement of one or more of the following five skills: Written Communication, Oral Communication, Computation and Mathematics, Critical Thinking and Problem Solving, and Decision Making and Values Analysis."[29] Closely tied as well to the education of undergraduates was the final fine tuning of an Articulation Plan in 1984. The plan was the result of a cooperative effort by the Ohio Board of Regents and the State Board of Education to assure the quality of the education of students entering college. The Bowling Green plan outlined a suggested high school curriculum and the requirement of demonstrated competency in reading and writing as a prerequisite for sophomore standing and of mathematics for junior standing. These provisions were scheduled to become effective with the Fall Semester of 1986.[30]

By the Spring of 1985 a reconfiguration of several academic units had occurred along functional lines. The long discussed merger of Journalism and Radio-TV-Film into one unit came with the creation of a School of Mass Communications within the College of Arts and Sciences. Simultaneously, the Communications Disorders Program was transfered from A & S and given departmental status in the renamed College of Health and Human Services. Two programs in the same college — Social Work and Medical Technology — were likewise made departments. The transfer of Radio-TV-Film and Communication Disorders from the School of Speech Communications led to the disolving of it and the conversion of the remaining divisions into departments; namely, Interpersonal and Public Communications and Theatre. The other major organizational change was the elevation of the school of Technology to college standing. In addition to these faculty based structural alterations, a broad spectrum of academically oriented student services were incorporated into two new offices; those of Minority Affairs and Academic Enhancement.[31]

The further assurance of sound educational growth came with the refurbishing and renovation of older buildings and the opening of and planning for new ones. In 1982 an improved Dorothy and Lillian Gish Film Theatre was rededicated with Lillian Gish present accompanied by alumna Eva Marie Saint. Also that Fall, the library was named in honor of former President, William T. Jerome III in a ceremony in which he took part. The year 1984 was marked by the opening of the first new buildings in six years when the Biological Sciences Laboratory Annex and the Physical Sciences Laboratory Building and Planetarium were completed. The following year, 1985, the completely renovated West Hall opened as the new home of the School of Mass Communications, and the entire campus was rewired with a new telecommunications system. As the university entered the seventy fifth anniversary year plans were well advanced for a $2.92 addition to the Business Administration Building and for major renovation of Overman and Williams Halls. These improvements along with the aforementioned increase in computer facilities in such places as Jerome Library and all residence halls gave added resource strength to many academic programs.[32]

A brightened economic picture in Ohio and the nation eased the start of the Olscamp administration. The nagging budgetary uncertainties and stringencies of the 1970s and early 80s were replaced by steadily increasing state appropriations from $67.7 million for 1982-83 to $87.1 million for 1985-86, and by a substantial decline in the rate of inflation. In addition, annual giving from alumni and friends grew steadily, and fees continued to inch up regularly. The latter led the BG News in 1982 to comment: "Well they did it to us again. Every May at the University, the Beta's have a race, Jed & Co preaches, UAO has Good Times' Weekend, and the Board of Trustees raises instructional fees."[33] A more solid fiscal future was assured in 1985 when the Trustees approved a plan to build an internal endowment fund through the process of defeasance of residence hall and University Union bonds. The program would by 2000 provide an endowment of between $35 and $40 million, the interest from which could enhance significantly various academic programs and scholarships.[34]

While much of a positive nature encompassed the early years of the administration of President Olscamp there were tensions. As noted earlier many faculty were disappointed that Michael Ferrari had not been chosen as President, and, therefore, were not enthused with the appointment of any other person. Olscamp saw this as primarily a faculty-trustee dispute, but recognized the position in which he was placed. In his opening address to the faculty and staff he addressed the issue by saying "The foundation of a successful university community, in the long run, is rooted in confidence based upon trust, not upon affection for the leadership of the institution, nor upon tradition alone, nor upon personal acquaintance or liking of individuals."[35] In the Spring of 1984 and during the ensuing year two major disputes occurred which strained administrative-faculty relations. The first centered around the announcement by the administration of a more stringent policy of solicitation within the university. The initial policy seemed to forbid open contact between organizations such as the AAUP and individual faculty members. After much debate a joint faculty-administrative committee was formed that developed a modified statement that was largely acceptable. During the Summer and Fall of 1984 a second crisis erupted over the rights and role of the Faculty Personnel and Conciliation Committee and the Vice President for Academic Affairs concerning particularly arbitration recommendations on tenure. Following some heated exchanges, both private and public and the resignation of some members of the committee, this issue, too, was assigned by the Faculty Senate to a special committee. During the Spring of 1985 the committee's recommendations were largely accepted by the Senate and the Trustees, and, thus, laid the groundwork for a smoother working of the entire conciliation and arbitration process.[36]

Despite some problems a number of positive steps involving the faculty and staff were taken. The most significant in its impact was the university decision to participate in the Early Retirement Buyout Plan of the State Teachers Retirement System. While requiring immediate retirement, the plan permitted the purchase of five years retirement service credit for qualified individuals, which increased their retirement pay. Some seventy three faculty and staff opted for the plan thus decreasing substantially the ranks of senior faculty; a situation viewed as a mixed blessing. The university also improved the Supplemental Retirement Plan which gave faculty and some staff the opportunity to work one semester a year for five additional years following retirement. These two developments affected various colleges and departments unevenly, but were accepted generally as having a positive effect. In a different vein, the rights of all university employees were further protected with the adoption in the Fall of 1981 of a Sexual Harassment Policy and in March of 1985 of a Racial and Ethnic Harassment Policy.[37]

Campus Life in the 1980s

The student body and the multitude of extracurricular activities characteristic of Bowling Green continued to flourish during the first half of the 1980s. Despite the earlier demographic concerns about maintaining enrollment, the university continued to attract students, although it took more time and effort to accomplish. The headcount was held at around 16,500 on the main campus which equated to approximately a 15,000 FTE count. The quality of the entering students as measured by national test scores and high school units completed rose slightly during those years.[38]

The typical composition of an entering class in the 80s, as determined by an annual survey conducted by the Office of Institutional Studies, was one in which women slightly outnumbered men. Of that group in 1982 54% of the males and 67% of the females said that politically they were in the middle of the road, and less than 20% of both considered themselves liberal. While 21% of both sexes had not determined a major, 84% asserted that they were going to college in order to get a better job. In the area of women's liberation 57% of the men and 58% of the women believed that too much pressure was applied on women to be liberated. On the issue of abortion the class was divided almost evenly in half. On one topic the class of 1982-83 was clearly different from its counterpart of a decade earlier. In 1973 73% of those interviewed declared that a meaningful philosophy of life was essential or very important to them, but in 1982 that percentage stood at 45%. The college student of the 1980s was clearly career or job oriented.[39]

Recreation and intercollegiate athletics continued to be popular. Among the top five reasons given for attending Bowling Green in 1982 the recreational facilities were fourth. Intercollegiate athletics experienced great highs and some real lows. During the 1982-83 year football and men's basketball and women's cross country and gymnastics won MAC championships while ice hockey won the CCHA title. The football team, in addition, played in the new California Bowl. In the Spring of that year the men's golf team also won first place in the MAC. The following year, 1983-84, the BG-Toledo Homecoming Game set a new MAC attendance record when 33,527 spectators filled Perry Stadium. The highlight of the year athletically occurred in late March when the ice hockey team won Bowling Green's first ever national NCAA title. The 1985-86 football season produced one more high point when the team was undefeated in regular season play (11-0) and won the MAC title and a second trip to the California Bowl. The glory and thrills of the year were dashed when Fresno State thrashed the Falcons in the bowl game. The 1985-86 year marked the end of an era for two of the majors sports, when both the football (Denny Stolz) and the basketball (John Weinert) coaches ended their ten year careers at the university.[40]

The Spring of 1984 spawned a new, but not entirely welcome, event—"Manville Madness." On Saturday afternoon and evening of April 28th a block party in the 100 block of Manville escalated into a melee of some 3500 people. While city officials did not overreact, considerable damage was done and some sixteen students were arrested. The event strained university and community relations, but led the following year to a major university "Springfest" held on university property with a much more positive effect both for the students and the community.[41]

The years from 1982 on witnessed some important developments in student affairs. The whole area of student life was elevated to a more important position by President Olscamp when, in his administrative reorganization, he placed it directly under a Vice President for whom it was the sole responsibility. This returned student affairs administratively to the position it had held under President Jerome. In the Spring of 1983 the Trustees, acting on a law that had been passed three years earlier, authorized the students to create a Student Legal Services Board, and to proceed with the hiring of an attorney. This was the culmination of a decade long desire by students to have a person who could represent them individually in legal situations. The service was begun in the Fall of 1984 with a self funded system.[42]

"An Environment For Excellence"

This motto of Bowling Green State University's Seventy Fifth Anniversary encapsulated the status attained over the years since 1910. During the seventy five years a concept and eighty two acres of land evolved into a university of 1247 acres, 101 buildings, and over 16,000 students. The original plan, to train teachers, demanded only a simple organization and a limited number of courses. But, as time passed, other goals emerged so that by 1985 seven different colleges offered 17 associate, 170 baccalaureate, 60 master, 4 specialist, and 9 doctoral degree programs. This proliferation especially accelerated after 1963, and was reflected in the sharp rise in the number of students, faculty, and holdings of the library, as well as in research grants and productivity.

Bowling Green over its seventy five years has faced and welcomed the challenge of attaining an environment of excellence academically, athletically, and in its student life. It stands in 1986 as the alma mater of almost 100,000 alumni, 80,000 of whom have graduated since 1963. They can be proud that their university stands fully recognized academically; that its colleges and schools are approved by their respective accrediting bodies; and, that its students and academic programs are accepted by all of the major national honorary societies.

The Falcon does soar, indeed.

Notes

Chapter VI

1. *Fac. Sen. Coll.,* Box 26-A, Folder 5, Min., Oct. 6, 1981.

2. *Ibid.; BOT Min.,* May 8, 1981, June 26, 1981, Oct. 9, 1981, and April 9, 1982; *BGN,* Vol. 62, #107, Oct. 7, 1981, p. 3, #120, Oct. 13, 1981, p. 1, #82, March 30, 1982, p. 1, #83, March 31, 1982, p. 2.

3. *CAC-HAM,* Box 106, Folder 3. Ferrari Speech To Faculty, Sept. 21, 1981.

4. *Ibid.* and Ferrari Speech To Faculty Senate, Oct. 6, 1981; *BOT Min.,* May 8, 1981, June 26, 1981, July 17, 1981, Nov. 3, 1981, Feb. 12, 1982, March 12, 1982, May 21, 1982; *BGN,* Vol. 62, #91, July 23, 1981, p. 1, #92, July 30, 1981, pp. 1-2, #109, Sept. 23, 1981, pp. 1 & 4, #123, Oct. 16, 1981, p. 1, #124, Oct. 17, 1981, p. 1, #45, Jan. 12, 1982, p. 1, #54, Jan. 27, 1982, pp. 1 & 3.

5. *BGN,* Vol. 65, #40, Dec. 7, 1979, p. 7.

6. *Fac. Sen. Coll.,* Box 26-A, Folder 5, Min., Feb. 2, 1982; *At Bowling Green,* Vol. 15, #4, p. 12; *BGN,* Vol. 62, #113, Sept. 30, 1981, p. 2, #132, Nov. 3, 1981, p. 1.

7. *MS-376,* #8; *BOT Min.,* June 26, 1981, Feb. 12, 1982, May 21, 1982, Aug. 24, 1982.

8. *BOT Min.,* Nov. 13, 1981; *BGN,* Vol. 62, #92, Aug. 6, 1981, p. 4, #140, Nov. 17, 1981, p. 1.

9. *BGN,* Vol. 62, #133, Nov. 4, 1981, p. 2.

10. *Ibid.,* #107, Oct. 7, 1981, p. 2.

11. *BOT Min.,* April 9, 1981, Oct. 9, 1981, Nov. 13, 1981; *Fac. Sen. Coll.,* Box 26-A, Folder 5, Min., Oct. 6, 1981; *BGN,* Vol. 62, #109, Sept. 23, 1981, p. 1, #107, Oct. 7, 1981, pp. 1-2, #133, Nov. 4, 1981, p. 2, #136, Nov. 10, 1981, p. 1, #141, Nov. 18, 1981, pp. 3-4, #44, Jan. 8, 1982, p. 2.

12. *CAC-HAM,* Box 106, Folder 4, NCAA Hearing Appeal, April 22, 1982; *BGN,* Vol. 62, #72, Feb. 26, 1982, p. 1, #73, March 2, 1982, p. 2.

13. *CAC-HAM,* Box 106, Folder 4, Ferrari Commencement Remarks, June 12, 1982, p. 2; *BGN,* Vol. 62, #83, March 31, 1982, p. 1.

14. *The Daily Sentinel-Tribune,* March 22, 1982, p. 1.

15. *Fac. Sen. Coll.,* Box 26-A, Folder 5, March, 1982.

16. *BOT Min.,* April 9, 1982.

17. *MS-376,* #36; *Monitor,* Vol. V, #25, March 22, 1982; *BOT Min.,* April 9, 1982; *Fac. Sen. Coll.,* Box 26-A, Folder 5, March 22 & April 6, 1982; *BGN,* Vol. 62, #82, March 30, 1982, p. 1, #83, March 31, 1982, pp. 1, 2, & 5, #84, April 1, 1982, p. 1, #87, April 7, 1982, pp. 1-2, #88, April 8, 1982, pp. 1-2.

18. *CAC-pUA 582,* Paul J. Olscamp. "On the Purposes of Education and Our (Undergraduate) Role and Mission." Oct. 31, 1983.

19. *Monitor,* Vol. VI, #15, Oct. 11, 1982, p. 1. Also, *BOT Min.,* May 20, 1983, Nov. 18, 1983, May 11, 1984; *CAC-pUA 554,* "President's Annual Report," 1982-83.

20. *Monitor,* Vol. VI, #15, Oct. 11, 1982, p. 2.

21. *Ibid.,* pp. 1-2.

22. *CAC-pUA,* 582 & 653.

23. *BOT Min.,* Dec. 10, 1982. Memo from Interim Academic V.P. to President.

Notes

Chapter VI (cont'd.)

24. *Ibid.,* July 23, 1982, May 20, 1983.

25. *Ibid.,* July 23, 1982; CAC-pUA 554. Annual Report of the President, 1982-1983; *Fac. Sen. Coll.,* Box 26-A, Folder 6, Sept. 21, 1982, Dec. 7, 1982, April 19, 1983.

26. *BOT Min.,* May 11, 1984.

27. *Ibid.,* July 23, 1982, Aug. 12, 1983, Oct. 14, 1983, May 11, 1984; *Monitor,* Vol. VII, #19, Nov. 14, 1983, p. 1, #41, May 7, 1984, p. 1; *Fac. Sen. Coll.* Box 26-A, Folder 6, Sept. 6, 1983, May 1, 1984; *MS-376,* #44.

28. *Fac. Sen. Coll.,* Box 26-A, Folder 7, Nov. 6, 1984.

29. *Ibid.*

30. *Ibid.; BOT Min.,* Oct. 8, 1982, Dec. 10, 1982, June 28, 1985; *MS-376,* #34; *Annual Report of the President,* 1984-85, Pres. Off.; *Bulletin, 1983-85,* pp. 20-21; *BGN,* Vol. 62, #110, May 18, 1982, p. 1, #116, May 27, 1982, p. 1.

31. *Pres. A.R.,* 1984-85; *Fac. Sen. Coll.,* Box 26-A, Folder 7, May 7, 1985; *Monitor,* Vol. IX, #1, July 1, 1985, p. 1, #2, July 8, 1985, p. 1.

32. *BOT Min.,* Aug. 24, 1982, Oct. 8, 1982, Dec. 10, 1982, Feb. 11, 1983, May 20, 1983, June 17, 1983, Oct. 14, 1983, April 13, 1984; *Monitor,* Vol. VII, #12, Sept. 19, 1983, p. 1., #37, April 9, 1984, p. 1, #39, April 23, 1984, p. 1, Vol. VIII, #12, Sept. 17, 1984, p. 1, #27, Jan. 21, 1985, p. 1.

33. *BGN,* Vol. 62, #114, May 25, 1982, p. 2.

34. *BOT Min.,* May 21, 1982, July 23, 1982, Feb. 11, 1983, May 20, 1983, June 17, 1983, Nov. 18, 1983, April 13, 1984, May 10, 1985; *Monitor,* Vol. VI, #46, May 31, 1983, p. 1, Vol. VIII, #45, May 20, 1985, p. 1, Vol. IX, #2, July 8, 1985, p. 1; *BGN,* Vol. 67, #122, June 12, 1985, p. 1.

35. *Monitor,* Vol. VI, #15, Oct. 11, 1982, p. 2.

36. *BOT Min.,* April 13, 1984, June 28, 1985; *Fac. Sen. Coll.,* Box 26-A, Folder 6, April 17, 1984, Folder 7, Oct. 2, 1984, Nov. 20, 1984, April 23, 1985; *Monitor,* Vol. VII, #37, April 9, 1984, p. 2, Vol. VIII, #15, Oct. 8, 1984, p. 2, #22, Dec. 3, 1984, p. 1, #23, Dec. 10, 1984, p. 2.

37. *BOT Min.,* Oct. 9, 1981, Feb. 11, 1983, April 11, 1983, May 13, 1984, April 12, 1985; *CAC-pUA 554, Pres. A.R.,* 1982-83, *Pres. A.R.,* 1983-84; *Monitor,* Vol. VI, #30, Feb. 7, 1983, p. 1, Vol. VIII, #40, April 22, 1985, p. 2.

38. *BOT Min.,* Nov. 13, 1981, Oct. 8, 1982, Oct. 14, 1983, March 2, 1984, Sept. 13, 1984; *Monitor,* Vol. VIII, #13, Sept. 24, 1984, p. 1.

39. *Monitor,* Vol. VI, #32, Feb. 21, 1983, pp. 1-2.

40. *Ibid.,* p. 1, Vol. VII, #36, April 2, 1984, p. 1; *BOT Min.,* Jan. 14, 1983, March 11, 1983, April 18, 1983, Oct. 14, 1983, April 13, 1984.

41. *BGN,* Vol. 66, #94, May 1, 1984, p. 1, Vol. 67, #117, April 26, 1985, p. 1, #118, April 30, 1985, p. 1, #119, May 1, 1985, p. 2, #120, May 2, 1985, p. 1.

42. *BOT Min.,* July 23, 1982, April 18, 1983, May 20, 1983, April 13, 1984; *BGN,* Vol. 65, #98, March 23, 1983, p. 1.

APPENDIX

Presidents
of
Bowling Green

Homer B. Williams	1912-1937
Roy E. Offenhauer	1937-1938
Frank J. Prout	1939-1951
Ralph W. McDonald	1951-1961
Ralph G. Harshman	1961-1963
William T. Jerome III	1963-1970
Hollis A. Moore, Jr.	1970-1981
Michael R. Ferrari (Interim)	1981-1982
Paul J. Olscamp	1982-

Board of Trustees

John Begg	Columbus Grove	1911-1915
D. C. Brown	Napoleon	1911-1914; 1918-1936
J. E. Collins	Fremont, Lima	1911-1920
D. T. Davis	Findlay	1911-1914
J. D. McDonel	Fostoria	1911-1918
J. E. Shatzel	Bowling Green	1914-1924
William B. Guitteau	Toledo	1914-1916
E. H. Ganz	Fremont	1916-1928
F. E. Reynolds	Wapakoneta	1918-1920
Dr. H. J. Johnston	Tontogany	1920-1935; 1939-1944
E. L. Bowsher	Wauseon	1921-1926
E. T. Rodgers	Tiffin	1923-1928; 1943-1961
T. C. Mahon	Kenton	1926-1931
Myrtle B. Edwards	Leipsic	1928-1935
Judge Orville Smith	Cleveland	1928-1929
R. G. Snyder	Norwalk	1929-1934
A. L. Gebhard	Bryan	1932-1937
F. J. Prout	Sandusky	1934-1939
L. N. Montgomery	Tiffin	1935-1938
Dr. E. B. Pedlow	Lima	1935-1940
Bessie S. Dwyer	Montpelier	1936-1941
E. E. Coriell	Bowling Green	1937-1946
J. J. Urschel	Toledo	1938-1943
Dudley A. White, Sr.	Norwalk	1940-1945
Minor C. Kershner	Liberty Center	1941-1950
Alva W. Bachman	Bowling Green	1944-1964
Carl Schwyn	Cygnet	1945-1965
J. C. Donnell	Findlay	1946-1965

Frazier Reams, Sr.	Toledo	1951-1957
John F. Ernsthausen	Norwalk	1956-1966
John W. Bronson	Gibsonburg	1961-1962
Anita S. Ward	Columbus	1961-1976
Sumner Canary	Cleveland	1961-1968
Donald G. Simmons	Perrysburg	1962-1978
Dudley A. White, Jr.	Norwalk	1963-1972
Delmont D. Brown	North Baltimore	1963-1971
Robert E. Dorfmeyer	Cleveland	1964-1973
Virginia Secor Stranahan	Toledo	1965-1974
Robert C. Winzeler, Sr.	Montpelier	1965-1973
M. Merle Harrod	Lima	1967-1969
Ashel C. Bryan	Bowling Green	1968-1976
Charles E. Shanklin	Milford Center	1969-1984
Norman J. Rood	Cygnet	1971-1980
Donald L. Huber	Trotwood	1972-1973
John F. Lipaj	Brecksville	1973-1980
Robert D. Savage	Toledo	1973-1979
S. Arthur Spiegel	Clifton	1973-1981
Frazier Reams, Jr.	Toledo	1974-1983
M. Shad Hanna	Bowling Green	1976-1986
Albert E. Dyckes	Columbus	1976-1985
Robert C. Ludwig	Marion	1978-
W. F. Spengler, Jr.	Toledo	1979-
Melvin L. Murray	Fostoria	1980-
Ann L. Russell	Milan	1980-
J. Warren Hall	Westlake	1981-
Richard A. Newlove	Bowling Green	1983-
Virginia B. Platt	Bowling Green	1984-
Nick J. Mileti	Beverly Hills, CA	1985-
G.O. Moorehead	Detroit, MI	1986

INDEX

INDEX (Con't.)

INDEX (Con't.)

INDEX (Con't.)

INDEX (Con't.)